COCO
Chanel

COCO
Chanel

Alice Mackrell

B.T. Batsford Ltd · London

To William

Acknowledgements

I would like to express my gratitude to the following people for their varied kindnesses and
help: Howard Batho, Rosemary Harden and Nancy Osborn, Victoria and Albert Museum,
London; Monica Brown and Beth Rhoads, Philadelphia Museum of Art; Penelope Byrde,
Museum of Costume, Bath; Mary Corliss, Museum of Modern Art, New York; Thierry
Devynck, Bibliothèque Forney, Paris; Diana Edkins, American *Vogue*, New York; Francesca
Galloway, Laurent-Charles Manoil de Brenaud, and Lucy Beverley, Spink & Son Ltd., London;
Marielle Guerard, Union Française des Arts du Costume, Musée des Arts de la Mode, Paris;
Pamela Harris, Christie's, New York; Andrew Kirk and Sarah Woodcock, Theatre Museum,
London; Melissa Leventon, Fine Arts Museums of San Francisco; Edward Maeder, Los Angeles
County Museum of Art; Susan Mayor, Christie's, South Kensington, London; Colin McDowell,
London; Charles McKay, Rochester, New York; Bernadette Rendall, Chanel, London and
Véronique Perez and Sophie Lorthiois, Chanel, Paris; Richard Robson, Castle Howard, York;
Alan Samson, Macdonald, London; Liz Smith, *The Times*, London; Pauline Snelson and Kate
Bell, B.T. Batsford Ltd., London; Eileen Sullivan, Metropolitan Museum of Art, New York;
Kerry Taylor, Sotheby's London. Although every attempt has been made to trace the present
copyright holders of photographs, the author and publishers apologize in advance for any
unintentional omission or neglect and will be pleased to insert the appropriate
acknowledgement to the companies concerned in any subsequent edition of this book.

CONTENTS

LIST OF ILLUSTRATIONS

LIST OF COLOUR PLATES

(Between pages 48 and 49)

INTRODUCTION

In his book *The Glass of Fashion*, Cecil Beaton wrote that two women dominated *haute couture* between the two world wars: 'Schiaparelli and Chanel. The first in time and by far the most gifted was Mademoiselle Chanel, a peasant girl from Auvergne who quickly asserted her forceful and unique personality on the style of the twenties.'[1]

SIMPLICITY AND ELEGANCE

What Mademoiselle Chanel gave to *haute couture* was a pared down and easy way of dressing, a look of classic chic. The ingredients are now what are called the basics of modern fashion: the three-piece cardigan suit; the two-piece sweater and skirt; trousers, jackets and shirts; and frocks, in particular, the little black dress, a fashion aesthetic that Paul Poiret called 'la pauvreté de luxe'.[2] An effortless style based on deceptively simple construction and workmanship allied to a palette of muted colours. For it was a style more than a fashion that Chanel produced and promoted. And no one was more Chanel than Chanel herself. As Marcel Haedrich, who was editor-in-chief of *Marie-Claire* when he met Chanel in 1958, has written: she was herself 'a Chanel creation'.[3]

An especially handsome, young-looking woman with a lithesome figure, Chanel wore clothing of her own design with great élan (**1**). With her slender figure and clean-cut good looks Chanel was her own best advertisement. She was admired and copied for her informal elegance as well as for her innovative style of clothes and accessories. She claimed to have designed clothes first of all for her own requirements:

> I set fashions precisely because I went out, because I was the first woman to live fully the life of her times.[4]

1 Coco Chanel in a cardigan suit of her own design, 1929.

Made of knitted wool jersey, the suit consists of a straight, loose jacket, striped sweater, and short, straight, slim skirt with pleats at the sides allowing for ease of movement. For Chanel details must be logical and practical – button cuffs must really unbutton and pockets placed exactly where you would expect to find them. Although a model version this cardigan suit could be copied by the ready-to-wear industry because of its simplicity.

Typical Chanel accessories are the two-toned beige and black airy shoes, and the costume jewellery of ropes of pearls, pearl earrings, and bracelets made of fake stones.

With Paul Poiret abolishing the corset as early as 1906 and creating his straight, loose, tubular Directoire dress which was easy to wear, some women already had a taste of freedom. But the involvement of many women in the war effort of 1914–18 had given them the experience of work and independence itself and they wanted their clothes to further reflect their new emancipation. Chanel felt that she herself personified this new spirit of independence and evolved a style of dress for the modern, liberated woman. Marie, Grand Duchess of Russia, who had worked exclusively for Chanel for several years in the 1920s expressed it well when she wrote:

Mlle. Chanel was the first to cater to the public in its broader sense and to produce a standard which appealed to every taste, the first to democratize the art of dressmaking for purely economic reasons. The post-war trend was for simplicity and informality. Chanel adapted it to clothes and she struck the right note.[5]

HAUTE COUTURE AND THE MASS MARKET

In the 1920s those of *bon ton* peregrinated around a yearly season taking in all the venues and activities of their class with clothing and adornment of paramount importance. Georges Lepape cited the following as the most appropriate fields for his fashion students to garner a knowledge of dress: '...sports, society, theatre, race-courses, salons, sports groups, airfields, golf courses, tennis courts.'[6] Lepape's remarks show that the major trend in the 1920s was for sports. There were also some new late afternoon and evening entertainments such as cocktail parties which took place around 6 p.m. and visits to nightclubs became all the rage. Chanel transformed attitudes to sports through her clothes, especially for women, and also put sportswear in the mainstream of fashion for daywear. Her little black dress was the essential garment for the cocktail hour. Those who partook of these activities, the well-bred, wealthy, leisure class could afford to by Chanel's original *haute couture* designs.

2 Four pieces of costume jewellery designed by Chanel.

Left to right: *a cross in Byzantine style set with six simulated cabochon emeralds with simulated baroque pearls at the intersections; a brooch in Byzantine style comprising eleven irregularly shaped simulated garnets and other pink stones set in gilt metal; a brooch of gilt metal filigree set with two simulated emeralds; and a white metal cross of coptic form engraved both on the front and back with saints.*

**3   Chanel cardigan suit
and costume jewellery,
1957.**

*Worn by the famous model
Marie Hélène, who epitomized
the Chanel look of the 1950s.*

However, Chanel realized that there were also fashionable New Women out working. Their war work had used up a great deal of physical energy and the natural corollary was to lead a healthy active life. Sporting activities were very much a part of their emancipation. Advances in communication, the explosion of fashion magazines, and developments in the cinema would guarantee that they were well-informed about fashion. While Chanel's *haute couture* designs were the prerogative of the rich New Woman, 'more or less clandestine copies were going to become possible, by virtue of the simplicity of the models, at a fraction of the cost and for far less wealthy women.'[7] Chanel considered this a compliment for, according to her biographer, Mme Edmonde Charles-Roux, Chanel was 'a creator of original designs who was only happy when being plagiarized by others.'[8] And unlike Paul Poiret she was astute in business affairs. Although he foresaw the vast market of the ready-to-wear industry and made innovations in that direction particularly in America, it was Chanel who not only captured it but catered to it assiduously.

ACCESSORIES

Chanel completed her classic chic with a group of accessories which complemented her clothing designs: two-toned shoes, beige with black toe caps; quilted handbags with gold chains; scarves; a variety of hats; black bows and white gardenias for the hair; and her distinctive costume jewellery (**2**) and (**3**). She showed women how to add flair to her costumes, for example, fake pearls or gilt chains with her wool jersey suits and fake jewellery on woollen sweaters during the day, something hitherto unheard of.

A FASHION FOR EXTRAVAGANCE

The name Chanel is usually identified with her cardigan suits and little black dresses. It seems to have gone largely unnoticed in costume studies that as well as these classics she also had a style for extravagance in the realm of evening wear. Her collections in the 1920s and 1930s were often rounded out with some delightful sartorial fancies such as gypsy dresses and heavily sequinned outfits. Chanel suggested that a woman 'be a caterpillar by day and a butterfly by night.'[9] She loved fur and fur trimmings, luscious fabrics and lavish embroidery that could easily rival the work of Paul Poiret, particularly in his pre-World War I phase. However exotic in feeling, these designs in form were pure Chanel. For luxury could never have any other purpose 'than to set off simplicity.'[10] Many of her creations evoked the spirit of art movements such as

Art Deco with examples of its very classic strand emphasizing purity of line and also of its sumptuous use of surface decoration. She also made some ventures into Surrealism (**4**). This aspect of Chanel's *oeuvre* can be linked to her appreciation of art and also to her playing a very active role in the artistic circle of Paris, just as Paul Poiret had done before her. She was a friend and colleague of, among others, Pablo Picasso, Igor Stravinsky, Serge Diaghilev, Jean Cocteau, Christian Bérard, and Salvador Dali. Chanel and Dali worked together in the theatre and she experimented with some Surrealist themes in her fashions. Her erudite article, 'When Fashion Illustrates History', which appeared in Paul Iribe's periodical, the *Revue des Sports et du Mode* in June–July 1936, shows her perception of the link between fashion and art. It is a *tours d'horizon* of art, fashionable women and their dresses from the reigns of King François I to King Louis XIII. However, she always considered the work of a fashion designer 'a technique, a craft, a trade' and chastised couturiers who looked upon themselves as artists. Nevertheless, her work can be seen in relation to art. The celebrated French philosopher, Roland Barthes wrote:

> Her work tells us (and she herself confirms it) that there is an 'eternal' beauty of woman whose unique image is allegedly handed down by the history of art.[11]

Like Poiret she also inter-related the arts. Her apartment in the rue Cambon, Paris, with its abundance of Coromandel screens, mirrors and beige suede sofas became a mode of interior décor that looks very up-to-date. She designed costumes for the theatre, her most notable work being for *Antigone* and *Le Train bleu*, which had a considerable impact on fashion. Invited to Hollywood in 1931 by Sam Goldwyn, she costumed Gloria Swanson in the film *Tonight or Never*.

LEGEND

Chanel closed her fashion house in 1939 with the outbreak of World War II. For any other fashion designer this would have been more than a full career. What makes Chanel unique and a legend that is not true of Schiaparelli or indeed of any other fashion designer was her astonishing comeback at the age of 71 in 1954. Chanel knew that the reign of the great male fashion designers, Balenciaga, Fath, Heim and especially Dior with his New Look, all of whom had dominated the fashion scene in her absence, could be challenged. To her they were élitist with designs that were intricate and complicated, out of touch with the social and economic

CHANEL'S IMMACULATE SHELL OF WHITE
GROSGRAIN. JAY THORPE.

4 Chanel's immaculate shell of white grosgrain.
Drawn by Marcel Vertes and illustrated in Harper's Bazaar, January 1938.

Favourite motifs of Surrealism were aquatic and marine life. The imagery of the shell had a seductive influence on Chanel's design for a hat in white grosgrain, a silk fabric showing a cord running from selvedge to selvedge. Chanel chose the perfect fabric, the plain white grosgrain giving fluidity and the cording echoing the sinuous, organic lines and curves of a shell. Just as the shell provides an outer, protective covering in the natural world, Chanel has inventively done the same for the fashionable lady with her delightful shell hat. Chanel has redesigned nature in a most creative way.

changes of women who were out working with not much time on their hands. Chanel herself maintained that 'I care more about the city street than the drawing room.'[12] She thought the time right to relaunch herself with a collection based on pre-war themes, especially the garment for which she was best known, the Chanel suit. She refined it again and again but never fundamentally changed it, consistency being the hallmark of her style. The Paris fashion world gave her a cool reception.

It was in America that she was warmly received. There, perhaps more than anywhere else, the New Woman had found the pace of independence most quickening and so it was inevitable that Chanel's relaxed elegance and understatement triumphed. By the 1960s Chanel suits were considered the epitome of elegance, and in the wardrobe of the American arbiter of fashion, Jacqueline Kennedy, who 'was wont to sneak off to Chanel...when she couldn't she had them copied.'[13] For the working women and the rich and famous alike, classic chic had come full circle.

In 1978 Christie's London held a sale of Chanel's wardrobe and costume jewellery. All the items were snapped up fetching high prices. The key to its success lay in the words of Chanel quoted in the preface of the sale catalogue by Hervé Mille:

> Je n'aime pas que l'on parle de la mode Chanel. Chanel, c'est un style. La mode se démode. Le style jamais.[14]

The beginning of the 1990s has seen a renewal of interest in clean-cut lines and a relaxed, comfortable and natural silhouette. Chanel's designs are as popular today as they were in the 1920s. This is especially true of her suits, of which there are multitudinous copies, and which are being worn by women in all age groups. It is a tribute to her that she was so in touch with the twentieth century that women of so many generations in tandem have worn her clothes. She never changed her fundamental belief:

> always to make yourself feel young – this means being free and easy and unpretentious in your clothes. You have to breathe and move and sit without being conscious of what you have on.[15]

The House of Chanel is flourishing today under Karl Lagerfeld who in 1983 was appointed design director for both *haute couture* and ready-to-wear. His collections have also seen some delightful and witty variations on original Chanel themes.

CLASSIC CHIC

LINKS WITH POIRET

Notwithstanding Poiret's 'la pauvreté de luxe' witticism, he and Chanel are perhaps the two twentieth-century fashion designers most closely linked. For both had as their baseline the natural shape of the female body. There are many reasons for looking upon Poiret as the catalyst of twentieth-century fashion. He abolished the corset in 1906 and had the hair of his fashion models cropped in 1908. He was the first fashion designer to inter-relate the arts and have a wide knowledge of specialized areas such as the Ballets Russes and the first to launch a perfume.

Poiret designed some very innovative fashions immediately after World War I. His firm belief was that dress must have a relationship with contemporary life. His work from this period has been misunderstood and is now fortunately being re-appraised.[1] It is reassuring to begin to read some perceptive comments, for instance that it was Poiret's 'dresses which founded the modern shape and style for women and opened the door later for Chanel', and, 'to the revolutionary shapes introduced initially by Poiret she brought the sobriety of masculine materials and colours.'[2]

Yet he was typically generous in paying tribute to Chanel saying:

> We ought to have been on our guard against that boyish head. It was going to give us every kind of shock and produce out of this little conjuror's head hat, gowns and coiffures and sweaters and jewels and boutiques.[3]

MOULINS

The story of that boyish head, for her style is inseparable from her

5   Gabrielle Dorizat wearing a hat designed by Chanel.
Illustrated in Les Modes, *May 1912.*

Chanel began her career as a milliner. Her hats caught the attention of the fashionable public when the actress Gabrielle Dorizat wore them in a play in 1912 and then modelled them in Les Modes.

Shown here is a typical example of one of Chanel's large, perfectly shaped and proportioned hats, made of black straw, with a huge brim turned up to one side, the only trimming a large white feather.

life, begins in the town of Moulins. It was there that Gabrielle Chanel was sent to a convent school in 1900, having been abandoned along with her two sisters by her itinerant-trader father in 1895, at the age of only twelve, at an orphanage in the town of Aubazine run by the Sisters of the Congregation of the Sacred Heart of Mary. The one nice by-product of her new convent school at Moulins was the friendship she developed with her aunt, Adrienne Chanel, who was also sent there. They both remained at the convent school until 1902 when they found employment in a small shop whose speciality was trousseaux and layettes.

By dint of their excellent training in sewing given by the nuns, they also managed to do some dressmaking for the fashionable ladies of Moulins. Moulins was a lively and prosperous garrison town with several army regiments stationed there, and, 'it was in a Moulins tailor shop that everything began for Gabrielle.'[4] The sartorial needs of the officers-cum-gallants were served by a host of tailors. It was during the horse-racing season that the tailors found they couldn't cope and the Modern Tailleur employed Gabrielle and Adrienne during these busy periods. Needless to say the charms of the girls did not go unnoticed by the impeccably dressed officers! Gabrielle expanded her repertoire of talents by trying her hand in the period 1905–8 as a café-concert singer and acquired in the process the nickname 'Coco'. On the stage at La Rotonde Gabrielle essentially knew only two songs: *Ko Ko Ri Ko* and *Qui a vu Coco dans la Trocadéro?*

> To call for an encore, her public simply chanted the two syllables of the word common to both her songs, 'Coco! Coco!' It was like a catchword that kept coming back every evening, every time Gabrielle sang. The nickname stuck. She was 'Coco' to all the officers, to all her friends in the garrison. That's how it was. She had no choice in the matter.[5]

ROYALLIEU

It was in this milieu that she met in 1905 a wealthy young officer named Lieutenant Etienne Balsan. He gave Coco and Adrienne the financial wherewithal to buy fashionable dresses to which they added hats of their own design. In 1908 Coco went to live with Balsan, now discharged from the army, at his magnificent estate at Royallieu near Compiègne. Balsan with his passion for horses had a superb stud farm. A life of leisure and luxury unfolded before Coco.

She met the wealthy racing set and a host of other people like the *demi-mondaine* Emilienne d'Alençon who was to wear Chanel hats and the actress Gabrielle Dorizat who was to model Chanel hats in fashion magazines and also to wear them on the stage. For Coco continued with her interest in designing hats persuading Balsan to let her use his Paris apartment on the boulevard Malesherbes for her millinery activities. Her career took off when she met at Royallieu one of Balsan's wealthy friends, the Englishman Arthur ('Boy') Capel. A handsome, charming businessman he was also a man of great intellectual prowess. The tone of Coco's life was certainly lifted for he interested her in literature and the arts. He was the great love of her life. 'He made me what I am, developed what was unique in me, to the exclusion of the rest.'[6]

CHANEL MODES; 21 RUE CAMBON, PARIS

Her millinery business had been expanding so swiftly that in 1910 Capel financed her next venture – her own shop at 21 rue Cambon, Paris – a street that is still synonymous with the name Chanel. Over her boutique was a plaque with the words 'Chanel Modes'. By now Coco was so successful that her hats were appearing in magazines. She herself appeared in the issue of *Comoedia Illustré* for 1 October 1910 wearing her large beautifully styled hats in black velvet – one adorned with a dark feather and the other with a white aigrette. The issue of *Comoedia Illustré* for 1 March 1911 featured a cover designed by Paul Iribe – who had collaborated so successfully with Poiret, and in the future would do so with Chanel – of the actress Jeanne Dirys wearing one of Coco's huge hats with a black velvet brim and cream crown topped with an aigrette. Chanel's work in the theatre, the subject of a later chapter, actually begins here. For the theatre at this time, just as in eighteenth-century France, was one of the main venues for showing off dresses and headwear, both by the spectators and by the actresses. There was a two-way influence, each aping the others' fashions (**5**).[7]

With the help of Capel, Coco's life and career had been well and truly lifted, and her modes continued to flourish. He also continued, too, to encourage her interest in the theatre, arts and music.

DEAUVILLE

The summer of 1913 found Coco holidaying with Capel in Deauville, a delightful seaside town on the English Channel coast. It was noted for the beauty and constantly changing nature of its light and had a long history of attracting artists from Gustave Courbet to the Impressionists to Pierre Bonnard. Capel persuaded her to open a boutique and again provided the financial backing. Naturally Coco chose the most fashionable street, the rue Gontaut-Biron, situated between the luxurious hotels and the casinos. Her shop

6 'Le vrai et le faux chic'.

Drawing by Sem, 1914. Featured in L'Illustration, *28 March 1914.*

This was one of Chanel's first suits, made at the request of Premet, himself a dressmaker, for a very much talked about courtesan, Forzane. Sem identified Chanel with vrai chic.

was on the sunny side so she put up a large white awning with her surname in large black letters – her first experimentation with the logo that remains to this day. She was already acclaimed for her hats which sold extremely well. Here she expanded her repertoire to include loose, casual sports clothes.

As per usual she started by designing for herself. Photographs of Chanel show her holidaying at Étretat on the Normandy coast before she went to Deauville. She wears a sports suit consisting of a long skirt and long jacket, very loose-fitting being made of *tricot*, and a white cotton shirt. She continued to be photographed in Deauville in these *tricot* sports suits, simply constructed, with the jacket having large patch pockets and a sailor-like collar, the provenance so obviously being masculine working dress. With its loose form that had no corseting underneath, Coco was at the same time paying homage to the natural shape of the female body, perhaps recalling the work of Poiret.

Another idea originally championed by Poiret was working on the live model. To advertise her new comfortable clothes she recalled her aunt, Adrienne Chanel and also called upon her sister Antoinette. They had model figures like herself and this was the beginning of Coco's working directly on the model, something she would do all through her long career.

Coco was also championed by the acerbic caricaturist Sem, a regular at Deauville. He wrote and illustrated a series of albums entitled *Le vrai et le faux chic*. The first one, in 1914, was devoted to fashion. He drew a lady as slender as the greyhound she was out walking. The lady in question was the famous courtesan Forzane dressed in a suit designed by Chanel. Sem portrayed Chanel as the fashion designer of *le vrai chic*. In March 1914 the periodical *L'Illustration* had an article on 'Le vrai and le faux chic' accompanied by Sem's drawing of Forzane wearing the Chanel suit (**6**).

Chanel's work at Deauville launched her on her career as a fashion designer. Just as she was consolidating her own distinctive style World War I broke out and the glittering set left Deauville. Capel, although called up, encouraged Coco to stay and his business acumen proved sound, for, with the German troops advancing, the denizens of Paris and much of the countryside moved West and the luxurious hotels of Deauville became hospitals for the wounded.

Ladies arrived 'having lost everything', they said. And it was true. Except the money to buy a new wardrobe. They went to the only shop in town that was open: Chanel's.

In return she offered them what she was wearing herself. A straight skirt just off the ground, showing only a glimpse of the foot, a sailor blouse, a shirt, boot-heeled shoes, a hat barren of decoration, nothing but a plain straw shape: that was her wartime attire. It was right for moving about on foot, for walking fast, for going places without problems, which is all anybody needed. The Chanel look became the look of the day.[8]

BIARRITZ

It is a quirk of fate that World War I not only boosted Chanel's fame, but also served her and her style and secured her future as a fashion designer. In the summer of 1915, Capel, although still in the army, continued with his business interests and visited Biarritz with Coco. Biarritz, like Deauville, was a fashionable resort, but being a Basque port, it had a Spanish rather than a British character. It had taken on a cosmopolitan atmosphere ever since the frequent visits of the Empress Eugénie. Biarritz attracted the super rich and those who were profiting from the war. With Spain, a country which remained neutral during the war, nearby fabrics were readily available and so was a clientele of wealthy women from Madrid, San Sebastian and Barcelona. Coco saw the untapped business opportunities at first hand and again with Capel's financial assets she established not a boutique as in Deauville but a veritable *maison de couture* in the mode of the great Paris houses.

She set up two workrooms: one the creative workroom where the designs were executed to individual specifications. Each workroom had about thirty people with a chain of command from the *première* down to the apprentice. Perhaps the most outstanding example of a Chanel-Biarritz design was the dress illustrated and applauded in the American edition of *Harper's Bazaar* in 1916 as 'Chanel's charming chemise dress' (**7**). The deep V-shaped bodice was outlined in delicate embroidery. The dress was beautifully set off by the huge plain black hat with a wide brim which the model insouciantly but flirtatiously tilts to hide her face!

31 RUE CAMBON, PARIS

Chanel-Biarritz dresses sold for 3,000 francs apiece and the chemise dress illustrated in *Harper's Bazaar* shows why Coco's order books were so full. Her work enabled her to pay back Arthur Capel and thus attain financial independence. She also felt confident enough to entrust the running of Chanel-Biarritz to her sister Antoinette. Coco returned to the rue Cambon in Paris in 1916 at first to number 21 where she had had a milliner's licence since 1910 and from 1919 at number 31 where she was officially registered as a *couturière* and where she would remain throughout the duration

of her long career and where the House of Chanel is located today.

Near the end of 1914 many who had fled the capital started to return feeling they would be a safe distance from the front. Some new social attitudes were already evolving among women.

> For them in the past, hotels had existed only as places for sin. Left to their own devices the abandoned spouses discovered that they could actually forego their husband's permission and dare to show themselves at the Ritz. They advanced as far as the bar, access to which had been rigorously forbidden them in peacetime ... Nothing could stop what the war was bringing women closer to, what had always been beyond their reach: freedom.[9]

Yet again the war proved beneficial to Coco and yet again she was in the right place at the right time, for the Ritz was also located on the rue Cambon a stone's throw from her *maison de couture*.

JERSEY REVOLUTION

Every fashion designer arrives at her or his own supremacy via a different route. Madeleine Vionnet, for example, expressed her exquisite floating, fluid style through her mastery of the bias cut. Chanel excelled at fabrics, their interpretation, and an ability to use them. That she could handle materials was also attested early on when she worked directly on her models Adrienne and Antoinette Chanel cutting the fabric with her scissors and designing and redesigning the garment with pins. Stories abound from her life attesting to her innate flair for the way a material felt and how it moved on the body.

That she was an innovator in textiles is confirmed by her introduction of jersey as a fashionable fabric. The name jersey in the sixteenth century derived from a worsted made of wool from the Channel Island of the same name. By the late nineteenth century it was identified as a close-fitting yet elastic woollen that was likened to fine knitting. Sportsmen wore garments made of jersey and fishermen wore jersey sweaters. Chanel became interested in jersey in 1916. By this time it was used in the main for hosiery and deemed unsuitable for *haute couture* by dint of its drab, beige colour and hard-to-handle weave. The textile manufacturer Jean Rodier hoped he would be able to use it for French sportsmen. But fastidious French athletes pronounced it variously too dry or too scratchy. Rodier was consequently left with a large supply of his wool jersey lying fallow. To say the least Monsieur Rodier was surprised when Chanel not only showed an interest in it but bought up his entire stock. 'It was exactly what she was looking for – a knit, but machine-made.'[10] The dearth of fabrics caused by the war effort and the trend toward simple, practical women's clothes brought about by the fact that women were working during the war in such diverse occupations plus the influence of sport, all provided a perfect opportunity which Chanel seized.

> In inventing jersey, I liberated the body, I eliminated the waistline (which I brought back only in 1930) and created a new silhouette . . . .
> To the great indignation of the couturiers, I shortened dresses.[11]

She had taken a humble material, one that was used by men and that even they had shunned, and turned it into a fashionable fabric. In the process Chanel also accelerated the growth of the ready-to-wear industry for it was a fabric within the financial reach of the majority of women who wanted to dress fashionably but were not well off. The March 1917 issue of *Les Élégances parisiennes* had a fashion article declaring 'le jersey est encore à la mode' and illustrated three jersey suits designed by Chanel (**8**). Chanel's combination of pure lines and plain colours often drew comparisons with the contemporary art movement, Cubism, with particular reference to the Analytic phase which ennobled humble materials and muted colours. She also dramatically shortened hemlines which had an effect on hairstyles for only the very short, bobbed style suited Chanel's jersey suits.

She was now becoming well-known and rapidly moving in artistic circles. Among those she dressed in her revolutionary jersey was Cécile Sorel, one of the leading actresses of the Comédie Française (**9**). One of Chanel's most enduring motifs was stripes turning the sailor look into something very chic and repeating it again during her comeback, a fashion idea that in fact persists to this day. Stripes, although they look simple, are, in fact, difficult to use on a material because the fashion designer has to keep the grain of the fabric the same in every part of the dress. Here they are handled to perfection giving Mlle Sorel's dress a distinctly nautical flavour.

British *Vogue* in its number for early August 1919 issued a clarion call based on its report from Paris. It published an article entitled 'Paris Takes its Summer in a Sporting Way'. What was called for was sportswear with clean-cut lines. Among those who sponsored this mode Chanel and Gabrielle Dorizat were singled out and the editor featured a fashion plate with this caption:

> Useful simplicity in clothes for sportswear is the creed that guides all Frenchwomen of today. Gabrielle Chanel has made a simple motor coat for Mlle Dorizat of dark blue *tricot*.[12]

7 Chemise dress designed by Chanel.
Illustrated in Harper's Bazaar, *1916.*

Unusual features were the masculine-style revers, waistcoat-effect and sash, all of these details as well as the tight sleeve-cuffs and flowing skirt outlined in exquisite embroidery. The beautiful dress is set off to perfection by the sable muff and another of Chanel's large hats, one side of the high crown decorated with sable, considered a most unusual way to use fur as a trimming.

8 **'Costumes de jersey'**
from Les Élégances
Parisiennes, *March 1917.*

*Three jersey suits designed by
Chanel. She brought about a
'jersey revolution' promoting
the humble material from use
as male underwear to high
fashion female daywear. The
hemlines of the skirts were
considered extremely short at
the time, and had an effect on
hairstyles. The hats, also
designed by Chanel, are, as
always, in perfect proportion to
the ensembles.*

She admirably met the exacting requirements espoused in the
article for the material was soft and pliable which Chanel allied to
her austere and unostentatious style. For other dashing sports coats
Chanel used tartan, another material she would use throughout
her long career and also quilting, which has become a Chanel
trademark being translated into handbags as well.

In 1919 afternoon dress and sports suits were still worlds apart
yet Chanel was beginning to find a market between the two.[13] By
1923 Chanel had done much to launch sweater dressing, the
sweaters worn with pleated skirts that were nine to ten inches off
the ground. British *Vogue* reported that

> the very short skirt at once suggests that the lady is dressed by
> Chanel who makes all her skirts short, whether for morning,
> afternoon or evening...the straight line is the medium of
> expression.[14]

In 1926 fashionable ladies were invited to travel by sea when

British *Vogue* featured two Chanel models on a yacht wearing sweaters, cardigans and pleated skirts. One outfit was a two-piece – a sweater that was fastened to one side with a row of black buttons and a finely pleated skirt. The companion outfit consisted of a plain blouse, striped cardigan with a row of black buttons and a skirt with the pleats this time inverted, a style of pleating that was very much copied. With the vignettes accentuating sports and healthy outdoor pursuits with plenty of sunshine all these ensembles required a slender, willowy figure like Chanel's. The ladies in the yachting scene are looking directly into the sun and one of them has the brim of her cloche hat turned up revealing her face. Chanel had been espousing a suntan as part of fashion since 1920.

Having discovered these comfortable, casual combinations Chanel stuck to them. The three-piece cardigan suit reigned supreme throughout the 1920s. It is well to remember that as far back as 1869 Charles Frederick Worth, the founding father of *haute couture* had created for fashionable women a suit worn with a shirt that was masculine in appearance. The term *tailleur*, which British *Vogue* had invoked in 1919, dated from the second half of the nineteenth century referring to a tailored suit or ensemble. Poiret designed some tailored suits and those in his post-war phase seen in such fashion magazines as *Art, goût, beauté* were in plain colours and made of fine wool. But it was Chanel who translated this into the cardigan, sweater and skirt or cardigan, shirt and skirt combinations that became classics and easily the most recognizable outfits in the fashion world today. She was her own best advertisement but she was also fortunate in having during the 1920s the promotional help of famous women. The actress Ina Claire, who wore Chanel fashions on the stage and screen in America, was photographed by Edward Steichen for British *Vogue* in 1925 wearing a Chanel suit. One of Chanel's most faithful clients, the Ranee of Pudukota, was photographed in 1926 with a caption describing her as wearing 'a famous Chanel suit' (**10**).

LINKS WITH MASCULINE DRESS

Chanel had been adding accessories to her costumes and in 1929 opened a boutique in her *maison de couture* in the rue Cambon, Paris, devoted to accessories such as jewellery, handbags, belts and scarves. The French edition of *Vogue* for June 1929 showed an attractive fashion plate of a mannequin wearing a plain wool jersey suit set off by a multi-coloured scarf and cap in a striking and boldly coloured geometric print. Her scarf and cap sets were surprisingly even taken over as fashion by men who used them in

9   Cécile Sorel in a striped silk jersey dress designed by Chanel.
Illustrated in American Vogue, *1 May 1918.*

Though quintessentially British, it took the French eye of Coco Chanel to turn the nautical look into classic chic. In the late 1920s, during the height of her liaison with the Duke of Westminster, she was often photographed in baggy, cotton trousers and striped cotton sailor shirts, inspired by the dress of the crew of the Duke's yacht, **Flying Cloud***. Just as she had upgraded jersey, this was another element in Chanel's canon of design, turning cotton clothing worn by working men into fashions for women.*

10   The Ranee of Pudukota wearing a Chanel cardigan suit.
Anon. original photograph, 1926.

Her three-piece cardigan suit consists of a checked cardigan jacket, pleated skirt, and long sweater with a belt and scarf to match. Additional accessories to go with the casual, elegant suit are a strand of pearls, leather shoes having two buckled straps over the instep and a cloche hat.

their winter sports. Here was an example of men cribbing Chanel's fashions, for the reverse had always been the case. It was French *Vogue* which emphasized Chanel's close links with masculine dress. Its number for 1 June 1927 ran an article entitled 'L'Élégance au Paddock' accompanied by a fashion plate featuring a veritable parade of Chanel models in her suits enjoying a day out at the races with the comment that

> never had her collections shown so many jackets that were so resolutely masculine in cut or so many broad-striped blouses and waistcoats or so many sports coats or so many suits and outfits to wear to the races.[15]

Chanel's adaptation of the forms and details of masculine dress are often considered in relation to dandyism, in particular to that archetypal dandy, George 'Beau' Brummell.[16] In the late eighteenth and early nineteenth centuries he was the arbiter of male fashions. For Beau Brummell sartorial impeccability was achieved by cut and sombre colours. Clothes must be restrained, precisely cut, and clean. The disciplined, unadorned yet very elegant silhouette was his creation. Chanel certainly espoused the Beau Brummell image and philosophy and can even be considered his equal in this realm.

Yet some of her early innovative designs in knitted fabrics did not have the sartorial distinctive precision of cut and tailoring required by Beau Brummell. She had a more general outlook.

Chanel had long been attracted to the English male wardrobe aided by her relationships with Arthur Capel (who died in a car accident in 1919) and with the Duke of Westminster. Coco loved perusing their closets and dressing up in their clothes. A charming photograph of 1925 shows Coco and Vera Bate, who introduced her to the Duke, wearing his trousers, jackets, sweaters, shirts and ties. What Coco liked about the English male wardrobe was its practicality with emphasis on comfort and good design which allowed for freedom of movement. While imbuing women's clothes with these elements she was able at the same time to enhance femininity.

Sem as early as 1914 had cited a Chanel suit as *vrai chic*, the model of elegance. Chanel was completely in tune with the twentieth century, understanding the changes in the lifestyles of women and also understanding how her clothes should cater to them. Chanel had brought about a revolution in daywear. She designed classic clothes that could be worn throughout the day and on a myriad of different occasions. All Chanel fashions were based on the natural shape of the female figure. Therefore she placed emphasis on an aspect where she could almost claim infallibility: fabrics. She always chose every piece of material herself. Whether young or old, anyone could look modern when dressed by Chanel. Jersey was in the category of materials that moved with the body and so she set about perfecting wool and silk jersey, especially its aesthetic and sensuous qualities.

Chanel used jersey on such a massive scale that she opened her own factory at Asnières, at first called Tricots Chanel and then Tissus Chanel. Among those she employed was a Russian named Iliazd.[17] An avant-garde poet of the Futurist movement and an erudite art critic, in 1922 he worked with the artist Sonia Delaunay on some textile designs. She was a Russian who went to Paris in 1905 and in 1910 married the great French artist Robert Delaunay. They both painted pure abstractions but Mme Delaunay was also interested in costumes and fabrics. In 1923 she worked with the poet Joseph Delteil designing 'simultaneous costumes and fabrics' to illustrate his poem, 'La Mode qui vient'. Iliazd's fascinating work with Delaunay caught the eye of Chanel in whose factory he worked from 1928 to 1934. He was first recruited as a draughtsman and in 1931 was appointed director of her factory with special responsibility for textures and colours of her jerseys and knitwear under Chanel's supervision.[18]

The period from 1926 to 1931, the time of her affair with the

Duke of Westminster, the Chanel style was very British, manifested again in her great flair with fabrics. Fine British tweeds also belonged to the category of fabrics that moved with the body and they didn't crease. For her suits she was also being supplied with a very distinctive English striped tweed for summer and winter wear by the firm of Linton Tweed Ltd of Carlisle, a famous company that was founded by William Linton in 1919. In 1927 Chanel opened a boutique in London with the fashionable English ladies giving their approbation to her tweed suits.

To be smart in town it was now essential to wear a Chanel cardigan suit. Besides her very influential jersey and tweed cardigan suits, Chanel continued to assert her considerable strength with materials often making her suits in very delicate, feminizing fabrics. A fine example is in the Metropolitan Museum, New York (**11**). The mannequin wears a Chanel cardigan suit, dated *c.*1927, made of silk charmeuse.

THE LITTLE BLACK DRESS

With her little black dress, Chanel institutionalized the *garçonne* look. The name itself derived from the title of the novel, *La Garçonne*, written in 1922 by Victor Margueritte which was a *succès de scandale*. A very racy novel, its heroine, Monique Lerbier, personified the emancipated, uninhibited modern woman. Key ingredients of the *garçonne* look or the flapper as it was called in America were the same as for the Chanel look: a youthful, slender, boyish figure, short hair, comfortable clothes and short hemlines. Emerging in the early 1920s the little black dress derived from the straight lines and flat planes of the chemise dress. American *Vogue* for 1 October 1926 prognosticated that Chanel's little black dress would become a kind of uniform (**12**).

As with the cardigan suit parallels could again be found in art. The artist Fernand Léger had evolved a style based on machinery and clear, sober colours. American *Vogue* drew attention to these severe little black dresses being all so much alike that they could be compared to the standard Ford car. They prompted Poiret's 'la pauvreté de luxe' witticism, extending it to 'misérabilisme de luxe', with the added accusation that women 'now resembled little undernourished telegraph clerks.'[19] The lightening of the corset, the purity of line, plain colours and stripping of ornamentation are all links with Poiret. Chanel overlooked all of this retorting that 'simplicity doesn't mean poverty.'[20]

There had been much speculation on whether Chanel's little black dress or 'poor look' had in fact any connection with the blurring of class differences and the expression of democracy. Some

11 **Three Chanel costumes, c.1927.**

Left to right: *cardigan suit in black ivory silk charmeuse; little black dress in wool jersey and satin; and a theatre coat in white and black* ombré *silk.*

see it in the affirmative and as being linked to her 'English hour', as the Duke of Westminster had a reputation for being socially unpretentious.[21] On the other hand, some view this as an

> over-simplification in the sense that Chanel's models were hand made from the most expensive materials and a mass-produced garment could never achieve the same effect.... The explanation, however, is not referring to actual garments so much as to the visual image created by the new styles.[22]

That she could indeed be an *agent provocateur* is proven by the fact that the cover of Paul Iribe's avant-garde periodical, *Le Témoin*, for the issue of 14 October 1934, showed the figure of 'Marianne', the symbol of the French Republic, in the likeness of Coco Chanel. Chanel's expressed view was to make her fashions filter to wide-ranging groups of women and she was the first fashion designer to do so. While the rich bought her *haute couture* little black dresses the not so rich could purchase mass-produced rayon copies which claimed to be light, comfortable and to give the wearer confidence and a feeling of liberty. Yet one has only to handle a Chanel garment, feel the material and see how it is made to know the real from the unreal thing. No one knew better than Chanel that a copy was only a copy and that an authentic Chanel garment could be easily recognizable. In *Kings of Fashion* Anny Latour says that Coco Chanel should have written a book entitled 'The art of dressing simply and paying a great deal of money for the pleasure'![23]

Speculation has been widespread, too, about Chanel's obsession with black. Introduced at the court of the dukes of Burgundy in the fifteenth century it has had a plethora of meanings in the history of dress. In early sixteenth-century Germany, in Spain in the sixteenth and seventeenth centuries, and in Holland in the seventeenth century black was worn by both men and women. In the eighteenth century English taste not only included the sporty look but also the sober black suit worn by the dandies in the circle of Beau Brummell and by middle-class businessmen and professional men – lawyers, physicians and officials. In the nineteenth century black became a male anti-fashion worn by the literary Romantics and dandies as well as the dress of the bourgeois professional men. Writers variously associate Chanel's predilection for black to her peasant origins, to her schooldays with the nuns, to her mourning for Arthur Capel, or simply because she liked black, thought it chic and would never go out of fashion.[24] Being a very artistic person with such superb taste the latter reason seems the most plausible. As she put it:

> Women think of all colours except the absence of colour. I have already said that black has it all. White too. Their beauty is absolute. It is the perfect harmony.[25]

There are various artistic parallels that coincide with Chanel's little black dress and together they express the age. As already mentioned there was significant work of the painter Fernand Léger. Black and white films were being made. In the field of photography the American photographer Edward Steichen, who worked with Poiret developing soft-focus photography for fashion photographs in the April 1911 issue of *Art et Décoration*, abandoned this style

12 Little black dress designed by Chanel.
Illustrated in American Vogue, *1 October 1926.*

American Vogue *announced 'here is a Ford signed Chanel – the frock that all the world will wear.' By predicting that the little black dress would become a world-wide uniform for women, and by equating it with the mass-produced Ford car, it recognized the beginning of the era of standardization in fashion. The fashion magazine might even have added Henry Ford's philosophy: 'You can have it in any colour as long as it is black.'*

for sharp black and white photographs when he went to work for American *Vogue* in 1923.

**13 Dress and 'Teheran'
manteau in beige jersey,
the manteau edged with
marine blue.** *Designed by
Chanel and illustrated in
American* Vogue, *1 February
1917.*

*The fashion magazine made
two salient points about this
ensemble: first, that to use
jersey successfully was a thing
few fashion designers could
accomplish, yet here it is done
successfully; and second, that
like many French fashions at
this time, the outfit was devoid
of all trimmings except tassels.*

COSTUME JEWELLERY AND PERFUMES

Costume jewellery was an inherent part of classic chic. Chanel
opened a jewellery workshop in 1924, where, under the manage-
ment of Comte Etienne de Beaumont she launched her *vrais bijoux
en toc*, that is, fake jewellery that looked real. Costume jewellery
was not an original idea of Chanel's. Homage must again be paid
to the pioneering work of Paul Poiret. He was the first fashion
designer to use costume jewellery in his collections. Poiret added
delightful pendant tassels, the 'tools of coquetry', to enhance the
two great themes of his dress; neo-classicism and orientalism. By
1913, the year of his fashion tour of America, 'Poiret-style pendants
hanging from coloured cords were being offered in department
stores on both sides of the Atlantic.'[26] That Poiret's orientalism was
still influential as late as 1920 is testified by an important Cartier
Art Deco diamond *sautoir*, having a stylized lotus pendant with a
tassel fringe, an idea gleaned not only from visits to the Louvre but
also 'from the fashion pages of the *Gazette du bon ton* which
illustrated the oriental designs of Paul Poiret.'[27] It is a tribute to
Poiret's aesthetics that as early as 1917 American *Vogue* featured
a Chanel outfit adorned with tassels (**13**).

Chanel herself had a fabulous collection of real jewellery, the
most stupendous pieces being Romanov artefacts given her by the
Grand Duke Dmitri, with whom she had a liaison in the period
1920–21 between Arthur Capel and the Duke of Westminster.
When she travelled, Chanel always carried her jewels in a sausage
bag. Bettina Ballard has related an amusing account of a train
journey she took with Chanel.

> She opened it that night on the Train Bleu and, to my rather naive
> eyes, it was like an Ali Baba scene. The train was hurtling into the
> night so violently that the jewels jumped on the table – a great
> jumble of strings and strings of pearls, necklaces of mixed rubies,
> emeralds, diamonds and pearls.[28]

Publicly, however, Chanel expressed the view that with her
costume jewellery designs 'women can have fortunes that cost
nothing.'

> Jewels aren't made to give people a rich look, they're made to give
> an air of elegance, or adornment, which isn't the same thing.[29]

Carefully placed fake jewellery, far from cheap as the sale of her
casket of costume jewellery at Christie's London in 1978 showed,
was an essential part of the uniform of classic chic. Whereas Poiret
had pioneered the original idea of costume jewellery, it was Chanel's

avant-garde way with it not to mention her usual deceptive simplicity and supreme artistry that made costume jewellery evolve into a successful and lucrative part of the fashion industry. Christian Dior put it succinctly when he said that 'with a black sweater and ten rows of pearls she revolutionized the world of fashion.'[30] The bulk of her most distinctive costume jewellery, such as the pieces of Byzantine splendour mixing real and simulated stones, the direct influence of her relationship with the Grand Duke Dmitri, emanated from her jewellery workshop under the responsibility of the Comte Etienne de Beaumont.

However, for her fake pearls she went farther afield. They are identifiable both by their unique lustre and colour – a frothy milky white or buttery cream. The mastery of this technique belonged to the jeweller Mme Gripoux who designed *Pâte de verre* jewellery for Poiret. She made *pâte de verre* for Chanel too and also Venetian glass beads in the form of large Byzantine crosses, probably the motif from the Grand Duke Dmitri's jewels that Chanel loved best. Today the Maison Gripoux still flourishes under Mme Gripoux, her daughter and grandson and still supplies the House of Chanel with handmade glass beads and pearls.

It was the unconventional way that Chanel wore pearls that caused such a sensation. One way was for day wear on her expensive throw-away cardigan suits and little black dresses (**1, 10, 11, 12**). This was daring enough but the aristocracy, who normally kept their jewels in safes and brought them out to wear with evening dress at court, must have thought all the canons of good taste were broken when she also adorned her black sweater with pearls and teamed it up with baggy cotton trousers (**14**). Although as early as the mid-1850s the American Mrs Amelia Bloomer had advocated the wearing of more practical clothing, in particular, a modified form of trousers called 'bloomers', and the Rational Dress Society, founded in 1881, had sanctioned her functional ideas, trousers were not generally adopted by women until the 1920s. Paul Poiret promoted the wearing of harem-style trousers before World War I but they were considered scandalous. Helped by the work effort of women during World War I when they wore men's clothing, Chanel in 1920 launched her masculine-style baggy yachting trousers and in 1922 her wide-legged flaring beach pyjamas. The 1920s and 1930s were the heyday of her wide, baggy trousers for leisure. Chanel's riposte related to Mme Gripoux: 'all those aristocrats stuck up their noses at me, but I'll have them at my feet.'[31]

Chanel's jewellery ideas were so original and had such an impact that soon fashionable women were wearing their real jewels as blatantly as their fake ones. In her stimulating book, *The Indecisive*

14 Coco Chanel photographed on the Côte d'Azur with the dancer Serge Lifar of the Ballets Russes, 1930s.

If avant-garde means to be experimental and to astonish, then Chanel certainly was with her costume jewellery, worn in a way which broke with convention. It was unheard of to wear jewels during the day let alone with sportswear. She has adorned her simple black sweater with rows of artificial pearls in a way that is still fashionable. Her turban-style hat with its twists and lines embodies the spirit of a shell, merging her **modiste** *craftsmanship with a Surrealist art image.*

Decade, Madge Garland recalled how one of the great classical ballerinas of the 1930s, Alicia Nikitina, was costumed by Chanel in the new vogue wearing a plain navy blue suit, the perfect backdrop for some sparkling jewellery.[32]

In 1932, at the height of the slump after the Crash of 1929, Chanel organized with Paul Iribe, who already held an administrative position at her textile factory at Asnières, and with whom her liaison was well over a year old, a scintillating exhibition of her own authentic white diamond jewellery designs. She had been asked by the International Guild of Diamond Merchants to create these original pieces. Held in her private salons on the rue du Faubourg Saint-Honoré, *Bijoux de diamants crées par Chanel* featured such sparkling pieces as necklace-collars with bows, bracelets from which rays of tiny diamond stones shone, and exquisite hair clips all displayed on waxed busts. 'At last, look what we've got, the real thing imitating the artificial,' quipped the spot-on Sem.[33] The exhibition was organized as a benefit for children's charities. Normally Chanel was wary of aristocratic society ladies and their beneficence. But on a higher plane it was another example of her munificence, this time to children. Sadly, she never married and had children of her own. She justified her choice of theme in this way:

> In my profession, the most diverse means are legitimate as long as they are used only in the true sense of fashion. What made me think of making false jewels in the first place, was that I found them to be free of arrogance at a time when luxury was too easy. This consideration no longer holds in a period of economic crisis, when an instinctive desire for authenticity in all things returns, and these amusing trifles are seen for what they really are.
>
> If I chose diamonds, it was because, with all their density, they represent the greatest value in the smallest volume. I used my love of sparkling things to try to conciliate elegance and fashion through jewellery.[34]

Chanel continued with her creation of fake and real pieces of jewellery calling upon the services of many prestigious artists such as Christian Bérard and Fulco Santostefano della Cerda, Duke di Verdura. With her flair for combining precious and semi-precious stones and with the inspiration of the Duke di Verdura she created some of her most innovative jewellery. Bent on a career as a painter the Sicilian Duke wended his way to Paris in 1927, his first job being a textile designer to Chanel. Coco was so enchanted with his designs for her fabrics that she later designated him her principal jewellery designer.[35] His first and undoubtedly most well-known design for her was a pair of bracelets in black and white enamel mounted with a motif of Maltese crosses made of multi-coloured stones. They were her signature pieces and she was rarely seen without them.

Chanel had a love of flowers and leaves and they figure prominently among her jewellery themes. Flowers were fashioned out of beautifully coloured stones their hues set off by a sunburst gold background. His themes and techniques, nature and the purity of design and colour, were often likened by his contemporaries to those of the Renaissance. One of his most striking and exquisite examples of the genre was a yellow gold brooch of fan design set with flowers made of multi-coloured stones, each floral gem giving the appearance of having been pressed into each gold petal (Colour Plate 1). The Duke di Verdura worked for Chanel until 1937 when he moved to New York. Like Chanel he was an individualist. The year of his departure Chanel was photographed by Horst P. Horst depicting her in her purist signature style (**15**). She is classic Chanel with her clean-cut, stark little black dress setting off rows of gilt chains with large coins, the cuffs of the long sleeves embellished with stones and gilt and wearing earrings with matching stones and gilt.

15 Coco Chanel photographed by Horst P. Horst, 1937.

A celebrated portrait of Chanel illustrating so well that she was the epitome of her own style. A simple, spare little black dress to which are added her carefully placed bijoux fantaisie and her hair tied with a ribbon bow – a vision of classic chic.

Chanel's good friend Misia Sert claimed some of the credit as the inspiration for the fashion designer's creating a resoundingly successful perfume business. The launch of Chanel No. 5 was in 1921 and the foundation of Parfums Chanel was in 1924 run by Pierre and Paul Wertheimer with the perfume chemist Ernest Beaux its technical director. According to Misia, a manuscript had just been found in the depths of a château on the Loire. It was written by René the Florentine, perfume-maker to Queen Catherine de Médicis. When Catherine arrived in France in 1533 to marry King Henry II she brought René with her. Misia explained to Coco the good fortune that could befall her if she could come up with a toilet water based on *The Secret of the Médicis*. L'eau de Chanel followed and Chanel 'had the genius to see the future possibilities of this new idea.'[36]

The technique behind the perfume Chanel No. 5, though, was the joint collaboration of Chanel and Ernest Beaux. It is thought that Chanel met Beaux, whose career had originated in Russia, during her liaison with Grand Duke Dmitri. In Grasse Beaux experimented with a way to solidify aldehydes, strong organic chemical compounds that had not been tried before because the formula was so difficult – the combination of some eighty ingredients.

Paul Poiret was the first fashion designer to relate perfume to fashion when he marketed his scents in 1911 under his daughter's name, Rosine. But his perfumes were based on easily recognizable floral fragrances. Chanel's idea was wholly new. She was the first fashion designer to create and sell an artificial perfume smelling of itself and not imitating flowers. An independent perfume for the modern woman – a classic scent to go with Chanel's chic clothes. Sem designed a poster for Chanel No. 5 (**16**).

Earlier with L'eau de Chanel Misia recalled that 'painstakingly we experimented with a very severe bottle, ultra-simple, almost pharmaceutical, but in the Chanel style, and with the elegant touch she gave to everything.' The *dominatrice* of understatement was making a strong fashion statement again. In the period 1925–27 three more perfumes were created by Chanel: Gardenia, Bois des îles and Cuir de Russie.

Anny Latour in *Kings of Fashion* posed the question: 'wherein lies the secret of successful fashion design?', and, answered in this way:

Secret No. 1: When a fashion artist – and this is pure chance – starts off from where a revolution is impending in culture, art and fashion. Secret No. 2: His flair for this coming revolution – and this is no matter of chance. Secret Nos. 3, 4, and 5: His talent in finding the formula for this revolution, his individuality which allows him capriciously and resolutely to stand above the fashion, and his intelligence not to let the means with which he sets the fashion slip from his grasp.

This holds good for Poiret as well as for Chanel.[37]

A TIMELESS STYLE

Chanel created a style for all ages. The understatement of her daywear also accelerated the growth of ready-to-wear styles. Its simplicity meant it could be easily copied. But Chanel herself believed that good *haute couture* should be copied. She even put to the test her belief that her designs should not just be the preserve of rich women but should also be enjoyed by their less affluent counterparts. In 1915 she also made up some dresses in the synthetic fabric rayon, thus opening up the possibilities of the use of synthetic materials and making her designs widely available to women. Rayon, in particular, which was perfected in the 1920s and called artificial silk, became acceptable and smart, and eminently suitable for the little black dress because of its excellent draping ability. Chanel was consistent in her principles, in the 1930s designing a blue and white dress made in British artificial silk which was photographed by Cecil Beaton for British *Vogue*. She also designed a sweater collection for Harvey Nichols and sold a dress and jacket to Jaeger's to launch their fashion department.

> This was a new departure and could be considered the forerunner of the boutiques so popular today.[38]

Through her egalitarian convictions about her clothes Chanel was not only advancing the ready-to-wear market and launching new ventures such as boutiques, she was also enhancing women's quality of life, giving them a belief in their own dignity and independence.

16 Poster design for Chanel No. 5 by Sem.

The model wears one of Chanel's chemise dresses of the 1920s. The Chanel No. 5 container reflects the style of dress – elegant, severe, unfussy. Made of plain, clear glass in a cube-shape design, the flaçon is free of decoration. Both items look simple and expensive – classic chic.

2 VARIATIONS

Comfort and functionalism have such an essential, definite place in Chanel's *oeuvre* that her name is usually associated with her classic chic garments alone. But as well as these timeless clothes, which must surely rank as her most significant creations, Chanel rounded out her collections with some costumes, mainly for evening wear, that are capricious, witty, colourful, elegant, very feminine and romantic. Cecil Beaton in *The Glass of Fashion* perceptively noted that

> Chanel's personality, like her designs, was something of a paradox. A mingling of the masculine and intensely feminine. Actually the concept she had of women was entirely feminine: she wanted them to be charming and simple and natural, bemoaning the fact that the young were not sufficiently romantic.[1]

Some of her fashions showed borrowings from ethnic sources, others from art, both contemporary and historical. Such a wealth of diversity with regard to themes, fabrics, and accessories was as usual allied to her formidable mastery of technique. Yet this aspect of Chanel's *oeuvre* is seldom even alluded to, let alone adequately discussed in fashion studies. Indeed, her own contemporaries and rivals failed to recognize her great variety. Notable examples are Poiret with his witticism about her uniformity and Erté who summarily dismissed Chanel as 'without imagination'.[2] It is Karl Lagerfeld who has done so much to resuscitate this side of Chanel's work. His insightful tribute in the exhibition catalogue, *Chanel at Sotheby's*, and the magnificent array of costumes shown in the London exhibition itself will, it is hoped, lead to more study. Lagerfeld recalled that when he was young he attended the Chanel shows at her salon with his mother delighting in their modernity, colour and sense of gaiety....He is especially inspired by some of her earliest designs – 'amusing, avant-garde, even outrageous'.[3]

ARTIST WITH FABRICS

Because Chanel was a highly intelligent person she possessed the ability not to take herself too seriously, defied convention and introduced humour into many of her fashions very early on in her career. In 1920 her *robe de crinoline*, a little black dress inside a mock-crinoline conjured up such amusement that even British *Vogue* was quick to spot it:

> Her crêpe de Chine frock was surrounded by a mist of black tulle, the mere shadowy wraith of a crinoline hanging bell-shaped from her shoulders. But when she sat down where was it? Vanished...with only a gossamer sweep left at each side of her black-clad slimness. Chanel can do anything![4]

It is interesting that for his Autumn/Winter 1988–89 *haute couture* collection Karl Lagerfeld designed a variation on Chanel's *robe de crinoline*. Anthems come to mind again in their Surrealist designs, Karl Lagerfeld's ready-to-wear collection for Spring/Summer 1991 featuring a similar jaunty shell hat fit for a Venus of the 1990s as much as Chanel's was for her counterpart in the 1930s.

Examples of Chanel's chameleon spirit are numerous. Her black tulle evening gown of *c*.1935–38, so light with its sheer balloon sleeves emphasized by the shoulder flounces, as if the wearer is about to be borne aloft is again witty, feminine, romantic – indeed fit for a modern Anna Karenina! (Colour Plate 3). Chanel's inventive spirit was still flourishing with her comeback in the fifties, for example, with her white and gold organza dinner gown with its dashing puffball skirt.

With her instinctive response to the sense of touch it is not surprising that Chanel should work with a very magical fabric, *ciré* satin, in combination with fur, renowned for its tactile qualities. About 1918 she designed a three-quarter length cape made of *ciré* satin trimmed with a high fox fur collar (Colour Plate 2). Lined in brown silk crêpe, this stunning garment bears the label Gabrielle Chanel Paris and the couture number 14000.

The *ciré* process involves treating a fabric with wax, heat and pressure and applied to satin produces a lustrous, smooth, shiny surface. *Ciré* satin is the material most associated with the fantasies of the 1930s, yet here Chanel has successfully experimented with it so much earlier. Her *ciré* satin cape gives the effect of liquid drapery its sensual quality highlighted by the swirl of fur.

Chanel's interest in fur went back as far as 1914 when she was adding it as a trimming to some of her suits (see **6**). By 1918, the approximate date of her sumptuous *ciré* satin cape, her fur-trimmed garments were 'making her a fortune'.[5] It was particularly during her 'Russian phase' that Chanel's fashions exhibited an abundance of fur. That Chanel's liaison with Grand Duke Dmitri proved very beneficial to her fashions was underlined in 1923 at Deauville where there was a spectacular display of Chanel furs modelled with great aplomb and elegance by a group of *émigrée* Russian ladies.

The 1930s was the decade of the craze for furs when they became the ultimate symbol of the social status of a fashionable lady. Chanel's early work had anticipated the rage and she now promoted their romanticism and fantasy during the economic crisis.

And the 1930s ushered in a new style of fashion illustration. Magazines like *Vogue*

> began to cater for the mass fashion market. The technical improvements in fashion illustration showed the reader and the ready-to-wear manufacturers alike what to aim for.[6]

Black and white photography in fashion magazines and films was so sharp, accurate and objective that the costumes featured could be easily copied and imitated by the ready-to-wear industry. In setting off for Hollywood in 1931 to promote her own brand of fairytale glamour Chanel was photographed wearing a tweed coat trimmed with a huge fur collar and deep fur cuffs.

EMBROIDERY

Embroidery has always been one of the pre-eminent ways of decorating fabrics. Historically Byzantium was the origin of the sumptuous hand embroideries that decorated liturgical vestments in the Middle Ages. Embroidery became a sign of social rank reaching its acme in the sixteenth to eighteenth centuries in Europe when garments were exquisitely embroidered with gold and silver thread and precious jewellery. Bourgeois society in nineteenth-century Europe combined lace and white embroidery work on clothes to assert wealth. The exotic costumes of the Ballets Russes in the early twentieth century continued the influence of embroidery as a fashion for ornamenting costume. As with fur, Chanel very early on showed an instinctive flair for embroidery. In 1916 *Harper's Bazaar* showed her chemise dress which was decorated with delicate embroidery (**7**). After World War I embroidery became a very glamorous adjunct to fashionable dress. The leading *maître brodeur* was Albert Lesage. He established an atelier in Paris in 1922 and in 1924 bought the firm of Maison Michonnet which itself dated back to 1860 and included clients from Worth to Vionnet. In addition to Vionnet, Lesage also did work for Paquin, Poiret, and Schiaparelli. Chanel, as was her wont, took a different route. Again it was an example of her lifestyle enriching her work. In the early 1920s her villa at Garches became an unofficial centre of Russian *émigré* aristocratic society. Her house at 31 rue Cambon suddenly had a master of ceremonies called Prince Kutusov and many of her domestics, and sales assistants were these *émigrés*. The lynchpin was again, as with fur, the Grand Duke Dmitri.

The first few years of the 1920s are often called Chanel's 'Russian phase' and many of her costumes are covered with brightly-covered embroidery showing Russian ethnic influences. They were the work of Dmitri's sister, the Grand Duchess Marie Pavlovna. The Grand Duchess met Chanel in the Autumn of 1921 in the hope that the fashion designer would give her some suggestions for employment. In her memoirs Marie recalls how the problem was solved quite fortuitously.

> A great part of her popularity came from the fact that the clothes she created were so easy to make; they were reproduced as fast as they left her workrooms. She had just then imported some multi-coloured Faro Island sweaters and conceived the idea of using their design for embroidery on silk blouses. One day as I came in I found Mlle Chanel engrossed in an argument with Mme Bataille, the woman who did the embroidery for the house. They were both examining the finished pieces of a crimson *crêpe de Chine* blouse. Chanel was beating down the price and she was speaking so quickly and volubly and had so many arguments at her disposal that Mme Bataille was staggered.[7]

After Mme Bataille not surprisingly disappeared from the room, Marie put herself forward as being able to embroider the blouse for 150 francs less even though she knew nothing about machine embroidery. She learned the technique of machine embroidery quickly and within three months was able to produce the requisite blouse for Chanel and soon opened her own embroidery workshop which she called Kitmir and 'had already an assured customer in Chanel.'[8] Chanel, in fact, asked her to quickly prepare embroidery designs for her Spring collection to be shown in February 1922. One striking design was her 'Roubachka', the blouse of the Russian peasants. Very long in length and with long, tubular sleeves, Chanel made hers in black crêpe de Chine and decorated it with Russian embroideries in bright red, yellow and blue. Besides blouses, Marie provided designs for tunics, coats and dresses. Even the ubiquitous little black dress did not escape! (**17**). One outstanding example is

17 Black crêpe dress with multi-coloured embroidery, designed by Chanel, c.1922.

Chanel has enlivened her spare little black dress with some carefully placed embroidery of Russian inspiration. The tubular form of the dress was an excellent surface for embroidery and the angular motifs admirably complemented its style.

18a and b   Evening dress designed by Chanel, c.1923–4.

Cream net over silk embroidered in an extravagant Art Deco design with pearl sequins and silver bugle beads forming a scrollwork pattern. The 1920s were noted for the practice of beading so heavily onto fragile fabrics that few are extant today. This dress is a rare surviving example showing Chanel's interpretation of the beaded dress.

embroidered with very small linear, criss-cross patterns in a multi-colour contrast.

The contemporary Russian Constructivist movement in painting and textiles also employed this design, the movement itself looking back to traditional Russian arts and crafts.[9] It was a design which would have suited Marie's machine embroidery technique since the motifs, being small and repetitious, would use few compositional layers, and meet the stringent production requirements of Chanel. What is achieved so beautifully is a symmetry and harmony between the embroidery designs and the dress which is unmistakably Chanel.

Some of Marie's designs looked farther to the East, British *Vogue* in its number for Early March 1922 singling out a Chanel dress in heavy black crêpe with a plain bodice and a skirt in an elaborate floral pattern in green, red and blue. Marie had a large library where she studied Chinese designs. One of her great delights and another source of inspiration was to scour the warehouses of Paris and one of Marie's great innovations during her time with Chanel was to re-introduce old materials into fashion and use them in new ways.

> Amongst these were chenille, which had remained forgotten since the end of the last century. I used chenille not for embroidery purposes but for crocheting hats, which Chanel was the first to sell

and which afterwards spread over the entire world. The first models for these hats were worked out jointly with me by a friend who worked at Chanel's, and then reproduced in endless variations by my own knitters. Thousands of these hats were made and sold for many seasons both in France and abroad.[10]

Marie's work for Chanel was successful beyond her wildest dreams. After about a year and half from starting, her orders had increased to such an extent that she moved the Kitmir workshop to new premises employing some fifty women in the workrooms alone plus a host of designers and technicians. Other important fashion designers in Paris began to approach Marie about working for them. During the first few seasons, fearing the wrath of Chanel, she refused. However, one day she consulted Mademoiselle which inevitably meant the end of their harmonious relationship. Chanel began to work with other embroiderers giving more and more orders to them.[11]

Although Marie participated in the great *Arts Déco* exhibition in Paris in 1925, there is no reference to her having designed the glittering Chanel dress in a lavish Art Deco design dated *c.*1923–

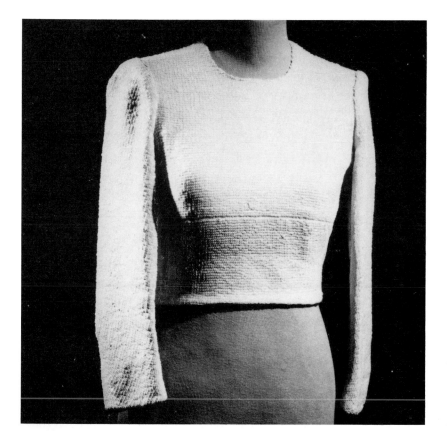

19 **Evening blouse designed by Chanel, c.1930.**

Embroidered overall with paillettes, this blouse was made especially for Chanel. After World War II she was often seen wearing it with a long white skirt.

*20*a and b   Evening dress
and jacket designed by
Chanel, c.1930.

*Shaped scalloped flaps appear
on the bodice of the dress, fall
in tiers on the dropped
waistline below which the skirt
fans out into a scalloped hem.
The jacket ends at the waist
with scallops on the sides and
along the lower edge. The long
sleeves have three scalloped
flaps at the elbow. All these
details serve to emphasize the
three-dimensional sculptural
quality with which Chanel has
endowed this outfit. It is an
extremely comfortable
ensemble with its easy-fitting
dress and 'throw on' cardigan
jacket, epitomizing Chanel's
philosophy.*

24 (**18**). The label in the left hand side of the dress reads Gabrielle Chanel Paris and the couture number 10660. It is a sleeveless evening dress with a short hemline distinctive to the period. An unusual detail is the V-necked mock-tabard. The tabard was indigenous to the Middle Ages being a sleeveless, hip-length overgarment used for military and ceremonial purposes when it was embroidered with vivid heraldic designs. Chanel has cleverly translated this medieval costume and its motif. The tabard, while remaining at hip length, extends enchantingly out at the sides to form a loose skirt with rounded corners and is framed at the sides with vertical lines of sequins and beads which merge at the bottom into a border scrollwork pattern echoing the bodice. The silk foundation at the hem has silver net edging and there are also side gores of the same net. If *haute couture* is distinguished by its exclusivity in design and the quality of finish then here Chanel has unequivocally achieved both.

The sale of the personal collection of Chanel which took place at Christie's London, in 1978 affords the dress historian a unique chance to study her workmanship and know-how. One outstanding example is her evening blouse dated *c*.1930 (**19**). Again it is one of her garments that looks deceptively simple in its construction with long, straight sleeves, a round neckline and fitted midriff. However, the seaming under the bust gives subtle contour to the body emphasizing a tubular effect which is unbroken by vertical darts. The label reads Atelier Mme Yvonne Guysleine, No. 38. She

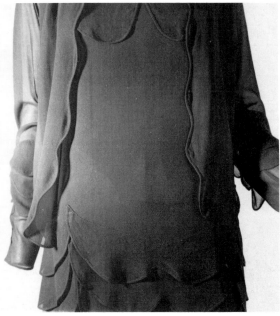

was Chanel's favourite model-assistant. Chanel wore this blouse intermittently over a remarkably long time, from *c.*1930 to her death in 1971, yet it is remarkably well preserved.

The two most costly fashions sought after during the 1930s were fur and the long evening dress. *Haute couture* continued apace, as Mme Charles-Roux points out:

> In 1929, while the United States lived through September's 'Black Friday', with its stock-market crash and bank closures, Paris, where the economy suffered less and the franc remained stable, entered a decade that for the *beau monde* would be incredibly luxurious, a time of splendid parties....[12]

The long, flowing evening dress of the 1930s was designed to show off a feminine silhouette, being cut close to follow the natural shape of the figure, gracefully outlining the waist and hips with the skirt flaring out.

And Chanel being Chanel went back to her roots creating, about 1930, an evening ensemble with such intensive attention to detail that it must have been considered the perfect example of her little black dress for the discerning eye of the 'poor little rich girl' of the time (**20**). The whole outfit is made of silk georgette, a material akin to chiffon. Like chiffon it is one of the most difficult fabrics to work with because it is so fine and semi-transparent. Both materials are very feminine and consequently need to be used in a very feminine fashion and draped with what Christian Dior in his *Little Dictionary of Fashion* calls *doigts de fée.*[13] Chanel displayed her 'fairy fingers' in this outfit with its graceful lines and subtle contours. Chanel's sheer technical ability gives a great deal of movement to the ensemble. An outfit of this quality can only be truly appreciated when it is in motion, seen on the shoulders with movement of the arms, legs and waist.

Who were the 'poor little rich girls' of the 1930s with the financial wherewithal to buy it? By 1932 Chanel had halved her prices.[14] Yet she still had one of the most expensive fashion houses in Paris with regular customers such as Barbara Hutton and Laura Corrigan who ordered twenty to thirty outfits at a time.

Taffeta is another material Chanel enjoyed working with. It is a fine but firm fabric woven from silk and noted for its glossy sheen and wavy lustre. About 1936 Chanel made an evening coat in black taffeta (**21**). At first glance the coat looks austere and stark. Yet when it is carefully examined there are some very interesting constructional details. The gored skirt requires a great deal of technical skill for it is a method of cutting the material into panels shaped like pyramids, making the garment narrow above, producing a semi-fitted top, while avoiding gathers or pleats in the skirt itself.

21 Evening coat designed by Chanel, c.1936.

This evening coat, made of black paper taffeta, is semi-fitted with a gored skirt and leg-of-mutton sleeves. The seams form a geometric pattern which gives a dramatic black on black detail to an otherwise austere garment.

Because she has chosen exactly the right material, taffeta, having an iridescent quality, produces with the seams a very unusual black on black detail. If this coat was not snapped up by Mesdames Hutton and Corrigan, it surely would have been by Beau Brummell!

Throughout the 1930s Chanel continued with her interest in sequins. Another of her plain black evening coats was decorated with them (Colour Plate 4). The details of the coat very much reflect the style of the 1930s with wide, straight sleeves, collar with wide revers, and padding throughout. The coat also affords another example of Chanel's labelling: Chanel, Cannes-31 Rue Cambon,

Paris-Biarritz and numbered 84.947. A black evening trouser suit, dated 1937–8, is so modern looking that it could easily be worn today (**22**). About the same date as the trouser suit Chanel designed a dress and cape of black satin embroidered with black sequins arranged in a fish-scale pattern, one of the favourite motifs of the Surrealists (**23**). Added piquancy is provided by the red satin panels and sashes. Red was one of the few bright colours that Chanel liked because she associated it with life itself. Chanel's use of red was always very arresting. Grand Duchess Marie recalled one of her most difficult designs for Chanel was on a light grey tunic embroidered in different shades of the same colour with dashes of red. When she saw the tunic being worn by a lady lunching at the Ritz she had great difficulty in keeping herself from staring.[15] Chanel's distinctive use of red as early as the 1920s was spotted by other fashion designers.

> Anny of Paris made women's dinner jackets on male models and added feather carnations in deep Chanel red for the buttonholes.[16]

Diana Vreeland owned the black sequin trouser suit. She had a love of Chanel clothes and shared Chanel's passion for red. She originally wore the trouser suit with a black ribbon round the neck into which she placed a red rose.

Fashion in the 1930s was also about 'the new economy' as British *Vogue* called it and

> for the first time cheap, washable fabrics are used for grand occasion clothes – Chanel shows a collection of thirty-five cotton evening dresses.[17]

LONDON

Chanel's business affairs in London steadily increased in the 1930s. After her brief interlude with Grand Duke Dmitri she embarked on quite a long liaison (1924–31) with the Duke of Westminster which put her firmly back in the orbit of British materials. In 1932 she was specially invited to London by the textile firm, Messrs Ferguson, to launch their range of cottons. She designed some delightful ball gowns and race gowns for débutantes and society ladies in materials such as organdie, muslin, lace, lawn, net and piqué. In 1932 the artist Drian sketched Lady Pamela Smith wearing a Chanel white piqué race gown (**24**). Piqué is a stiff ribbed cotton material yet exquisite details such as the floral trim cut off the sleeves and skirt to give the gown a fluidity of movement that says Chanel.

Through the munificent loan by the Duke of Westminster of his

22 **Black sequin evening trouser suit designed by Chanel, 1936–7.**

Opposite left: *The sequins which entirely cover this suit have a very metallic sheen and sharply outline the detail of the ensemble. The trousers hang from a yoke at the hips, the careful seaming of the wide waistband providing a long, slim, column-like sleekness. The bolero is short, ending well above the waistline, open, and loose-fitting. Of Spanish origin, this jacket was one of the most fashionable garments of the 1930s.*

23 **Evening dress and cape designed by Chanel, 1937–8.**

Opposite right: *The black satin dress with its glistening black sequins applied in a fish-scale pattern, a favourite motif of the Surrealists, and bright satin panels is particularly striking. The dress is sleeveless, the bodice having a low décolletage and narrow straps. The black satin cape is also decorated with black sequins and has small revers in red satin. Lined in red satin, the cape is short and semi-circular in shape falling in soft, fluid folds over the shoulders and can be closed at the neck by a hook fastening.*

24   Lady Pamela Smith in a race gown of white piqué trimmed with a flower garland of the same material designed by Chanel, 1932. *Sketch by Drian.*

Chanel was invited to London by Messrs Ferguson to launch English cottons in fashion. She created an enchanting collection of race gowns and ball gowns for fashionable English society ladies. Chanel also held a benefit show of her designs all modelled by non-professionals including Lady Pamela Smith.

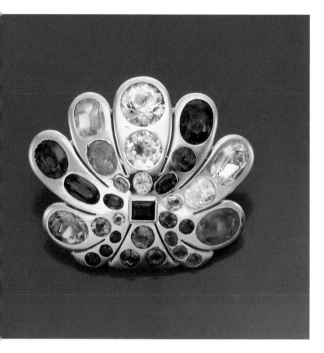

1 (Above) Precious, semi-precious gem and yellow gold brooch. Signed by Chanel. Of fan design, the centre is set with a rectangular-cut blue sapphire, surrounded by circular and oval-cut green tourmalines, blue sapphires, citrines, garnets, aquamarines, light yellow orthoclase feldspar, rock crystal, pink tourmalines and pink sapphires mounted in gold. While the brooch bears the Chanel signature, it was almost certainly designed by Fulco Santostefano della Cerda, Duke di Verdura.

2 (Right) Cape designed by Chanel, c1918. This three-quarter length cape is made of ciré black satin and is trimmed with a high fox-fur collar. The waist is dropped and slightly elasticated at the hips to give a balloon-like effect which is further accentuated by the position of the arms which slip through the lining to hold the cape in place. The lining is made of brown silk crêpe.

4 *(Below) Sequinned evening coat designed by Chanel, 1930s. This black coat exemplifies the style of the 1930s with its shimmering, metallic sheen, wide, straight sleeves, collar with wide revers, and padding throughout. It is lined in black crêpe de Chine.*

3 *(Above) Black tulle evening gown designed by Chanel, c1935-38. Chanel's graceful concoction evokes the nineteenth-century romantic silhouette with its balloon sleeves, the ethereal spirit emphasized by the flounces fluting the shoulders and the long, wide, full skirt. Also suited to this picturesque revival are the jewels used as buttons on the corsage of the dress becoming part of the gown.*

5 (Below) Chanel dress and headdress drawn by Christian Bérard. Illustrated in American Vogue, 15 March 1938. The dress is made of light green tulle with red flowers and has a matching floating scarf. The headdress is made of the same fabric and has a large black velvet bow at the nape of the neck.

6 (Above) Black and gold-flecked evening gown, designed by Chanel, c1959. This dramatic gown is shirred overall and embellished with bold black and gold bows and ribbons.

7 *(Right) Two suits designed by Chanel. (Left) The jacket and skirt are made of pink angora twill and are worn with a multi-coloured chiné-printed silk taffeta blouse with a self-tie at the neck, c.1960. (Right) The jacket and skirt are made of ivory raw silk. The skirt is unusual with its apron-like style. The layering on the skirt is echoed in the collar, cuffs, pockets and revers of the jacket, 1963.*

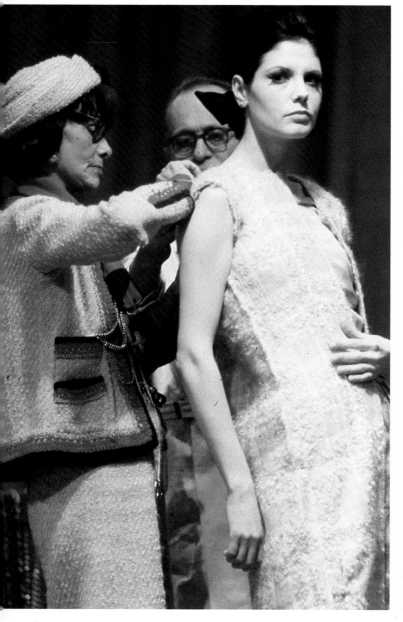

8 *(Left) Chanel makes a final adjustment to a model's costume before allowing her onto the catwalk.*

9 (Below) Printed mohair and silk tweed suit designed by Chanel, 1968. The suit is printed in bright green, orange and turquoise on an ivory ground. The jacket has a side fastening and is outlined with gold chains, making jewellery a component of the garment itself.

10 (Above) Autumn/Winter 1987-88 Haute Couture Collection. Karl Lagerfeld for Chanel. Inés de la Fressange wears a little black dress, a Chanel classic. Typically, Lagerfeld has made the queen of the wardrobe modern, with a short, tight silhouette and minimal decoration of large gold buttons. An insouciant but dramatic touch is provided by a large black hat.

11 *(Opposite page) Autumn/Winter 1985-86 Haute Couture. Karl Lagerfeld for Chanel. In 1983 Karl Lagerfeld maintained that the shape of the female body of the 1980s was different from that of the 1950s, the 1980s emphasis being on shoulders, a long waist, hips that are not round and long legs. Corresponding with this was a change in posture and movement. In this striking black dress with its imaginative use of gold buttons and matching scarf, proportions are in scale and the lines are sleek and supple.*

12 *(Left) Autumn/Winter 1991-92 Ready-to-Wear. Karl Lagerfeld for Chanel. Karl Lagerfeld's upbeat prêt-à-porter line for Chanel has emphatically established the short, floaty skirt made in a light, soft fabric worn under a curvy, fitted long jacket decorated with gold buttons and dangling gold chains. An arty, graphic block of red, Lagerfeld has made the Chanel suit young, fresh and fun for the beginning of the 1990s producing a new shape while still retaining the identification that says Chanel.*

Chanel dines at home
in printed pyjamas,
sweater, barbaric jewels.
(Two small Chanels)
Striped linen, flannel jacket.
Checked tussur, chiffon cape-veil.

13 *Clothes designed and worn by Coco Chanel. Gouache by Christian Bérard from* American Vogue, *7 July 1937.*
Here he sums up the essence of Chanel's fashions.

stately apartments in Grosvenor Square, London, Chanel in May 1932 organized another of her benefit shows, this time of some one hundred and thirty creations all made in British materials. All the costumes were modelled by non-professionals, one of the most notable socialites being the *soignée* Lady Pamela Smith. The *Daily Mail* enthused about the event:

> It draws from five to six hundred people a day and manufacturers from all countries are rushing to see it. Many visitors bring their own dressmakers, for this collection is not intended for sale. Mademoiselle Chanel has authorized the designs to be copied.[18]

FASHION INTO ART

During the last years of the 1930s Chanel brought about a fascinating interplay between fashion and art. The most topical art movement of the 1930s and the one that dominated fashion and fashion illustration was Surrealism. Chanel, as we have already seen, was very much the artistic fashion designer bringing creativity especially to the Surrealist vision of marine and aquatic life with her shell hat (**4**) and the use of the fish-scale pattern (**23**). With verve and vivacity she continued to sustain this theme in her fashions well beyond the heyday of Surrealism. Yet it is often assumed that Surrealism and fashion was the sole domain of one fashion designer, Elsa Schiaparelli.

> While Coco Chanel, her greatest rival, was designing fashionable dress for the new emancipated women, and adhered to the philosophy of the Bauhaus School of Design, 'Form Follows Fashion', Schiaparelli was creating fashion inspired by, and in collaboration with, the avant-garde artists of the day, Dali, Cocteau, Beaumont.[19]

Chanel was a very close friend of both Dali and Cocteau. She was also a member of their artistic circle collaborating with them on costume designs for a whole host of ballets and plays (see Chapter 3). It was inevitable that she ventured into Surrealism. One of the great graphic artists of Surrealism, Edouard Benito, in fact saw the fashions of Chanel and Schiaparelli as perfect foils that could be used to great advantage in evoking the mysterious, dream world of Surrealism. During the 1930s fashion and fashion illustration enjoyed a special relationship with Surrealism. One theme of the Surrealists was the quest for a metaphor for the human body which found expression in bizarre but fashionably dressed models (**25**). Benito's haunting drawing of two statuary mannequins carrying their own heads, one attired in a Chanel black lace evening dress and the other in a Schiaparelli wine crêpe evening suit with leg-

25 **Drawing of a Chanel black lace evening gown and a Schiaparelli wine crêpe evening suit by Edouard Benito.** *Illustrated in American* Vogue, *15 July 1938.*

Chanel considered Schiaparelli her great nemesis and the feeling was mutual. It was highly unusual, to say the least, to find their fashions illustrated together. In this sketch Benito has made the two rival fashion designers collaborators in the evocation of Surrealist mannequins, wittily and cleverly placing them within a Surrealist landscape.

of-mutton sleeves appeared in the issue of American *Vogue* for 15 July 1938.

Even though they were great rivals and couldn't bear one another, Chanel calling Schiaparelli 'that Italian who makes clothes' and Schiaparelli calling Chanel 'that dreary little bourgeoise', they were not above keeping an eye on each other's fashions, Surrealist and otherwise.[20] Schiaparelli 'followed in Chanel's footsteps and came to an agreement with an English manufacturer to design blouses and sports clothes for the new fabric Viyella', while early in 1950 Schiaparelli's 'lamé-bound cellophane X-ray cardigan and sheath dress was noticed by no one except Chanel, who brought it out in overskirts as an 'original' several years later.'[21]

During the last years of the 1930s Chanel also drew on art historical sources of the eighteenth century for her fashions. American *Vogue* in its number for 15 March 1938 featured a dress it called 'Chanel's eighteenth-century fantasy'[22] which was the work of the artist Christian Bérard (Colour Plate 5). In addition to being a painter he is well-known for his stage and costume designs for many plays and ballets, especially those of Jean Cocteau. During the 1930s he also turned his artistry to fabrics and fashion illustration. When he made his drawing for *Vogue* he immediately linked Chanel's design with one eighteenth-century painter,

26 Chanel with her model Muriel Maxwell wearing a black silk velvet Watteau suit and hat, white frilly neck ruff and cuffs and white silk gloves. *Photograph by Horst P. Horst. Published in American* Vogue, *15 September 1939.*

'The Velvet Touch' proclaimed the fashion magazine, 'Chanel's eye rests approvingly on the pinched waist of her velvet Watteau suit.' One trend, unusual for Chanel, that emerged on the eve of World War II, was her wasp-waisted costume.

François Boucher (1703–1770). One of the great Rococo artists, Boucher's paintings are characterized by asymetrical curves, prettiness and gaiety. Bérard placed Chanel's model in the centre of a very Boucheresque frame surrounded by four angels whose costume echoes her own. The shape and form of the work evoked the elegant, free, light, vapoury style of Boucher.

World War II had already been declared when American *Vogue* published Chanel's most celebrated use of art historicism, her Watteau suit (**26**). The ensemble was called a Watteau suit because it resembled the black suit worn by many women in the paintings in the early eighteenth century of Jean-Antoine Watteau (1684–1721).[23] Watteau attired his ladies in a suit made of black silk velvet having a long, full skirt and a jacket with long, tight sleeves and featuring a minute waist that was very tightly corseted.

It is curious that at the beginning of World War II Chanel should present a tiny, tightly-cinched waist and full skirt. It is equally curious that the first post-World War II fashion to emerge was Christian Dior's New Look featuring a tight-waist and full skirt. When Karl Lagerfeld showed his collection for Chanel in July 1989 it was dubbed a modern version of Dior's New Look. Lagerfeld replied:

> but it wasn't the New Look. It was inspired by Coco Chanel's 1939 collection that was never shown. She got there first and I've got the documents to prove it.[24]

And we have Horst's photograph. In the photograph Chanel is seen seated behind Muriel Maxwell ostensibly examining her Watteau suit. But Chanel peers out most hauntingly and introspectively as if she is looking beyond.

Chanel's Watteau suit must surely rank as one of her most ethereal and beautiful creations. It would have been interesting to see what direction Chanel's fashions would have taken after it was shown. But political events overtook those of fashion. With the onset of war, Chanel, alas, closed down her fashion house. Only her boutique devoted to accessories and perfumes remained open.

3 THEATRE AND FILMS

Actresses, as we have seen, contributed much to the success of Chanel as a fashion designer. She had met Gabrielle Dorizat in the fun-loving society of Etienne Balsan at the Château de Royallieu. In 1912 Mlle Dorizat wore Chanel hats on the stage in Paris and also modelled them in *Les Modes*, one of the most influential fashion periodicals before World War I (see **5**). Cécile Sorel wore some of Chanel's dresses in the play *L'Abbé Constantin*, and also modelled them in the 1 May 1918 issue of American *Vogue*. Chanel had been introduced to Mlle Sorel in 1914 by the Baronne de Rothschild, on the wave of the Baronne's celebrated row with Paul Poiret.

THE CIRCLE OF MISIA, DIAGHILEV AND COCTEAU

It was in fact a dinner party given by Cécile Sorel that marked the decisive turning point of Chanel's entry into not only high society but also into the artistic world of Paris. Paul Morand recorded in his diary the precise date of the momentous occasion: 30 May 1917. Present at the party was Misia Sert upon whom Chanel made a very favourable impression.

> She seemed to me gifted with infinite grace and when, as we were saying goodnight, I admired her ravishing fur-trimmed red velvet coat, she took it off and put it on my shoulders, saying with charming spontaneity that she would only be too happy to give it to me.[1]

Although she thought Chanel's gesture lovely Misia couldn't accept the beautiful coat. But she was bewitched by Chanel and couldn't wait until the next day to visit her in the rue Cambon. Chanel had met the only woman who would ever have any influence upon her and 'for thirty years, she was associated with the thoughts, judgements, and tastes of a woman known to have had a share in

27 Sketch of Chanel *by Jean Cocteau, 1937.*

Chanel's evening dress bears her trademark style – collarless, with jewellery trimmings and a bow in the hair.

every artistic activity of her age.'[2]

Of Polish origin, Misia's influence lay in her good looks and charm, and in her talent as a pianist. Liszt, Debussy and Ravel were among those for whom she had played. But it was her string of marriages that catapulted her into the artistic world and high society of Paris. In 1893 she married Thadée Natanson, editor of *La Revue blanche*, the bi-monthly periodical of the intellectual avant-garde in Paris. Lithographic posters promoting the journal were produced by Natanson's friends Edouard Vuillard, Pierre Bonnard and Henri de Toulouse-Lautrec. Without fail they took Misia as their model.

Misia was identified as the spirit, indeed, the symbol of *La Revue blanche*. Among the artists who contributed illustrations to the magazine was Pierre-Auguste Renoir. He painted a whole series of portraits of Misia including the stunning one of 1904 in the collection of the National Gallery, London. It was painted on the eve of her marriage to husband number two, the wealthy publisher Alfred Edwards (**28**). Misia wears an elaborate formal evening dress. The dress has a low, round neckline and short, full sleeves. While the waist is tight-fitting, the fullness across the bust gives a soft, pouched effect accentuated by the centrally-placed large, black bow. The pale pink bodice is set off by a full skirt in a dazzling print of white, black, red and yellow tones. The general effect is one of soft, undulating curves.

By the time Misia met Chanel she was living with a Spanish painter, José-Maria Sert, who became husband number three in 1920. By now Misia was quite celebrated with her circle extending to the Cubist painters, in particular Pablo Picasso, Juan Gris and Georges Braque, to Serge Diaghilev of the Ballets Russes, and to Jean Cocteau, the artist, playwright, poet and stage designer who worked with Diaghilev on a number of his ballets. Misia wrote:

> Coco came to know Diaghilev at my house, as well as the whole group of artists who gravitated around the Ballets Russes. And they found in her a faithful, very generous friend. Stravinsky in particular fell desperately in love with her! Afterwards, she was to give him a house in Garches and frequently, financial help too.[3]

In 1920 Chanel began her role as patroness of the arts. Boris Kochno, Diaghilev's secretary and artistic adviser to the Ballets Russes, divulged long afterwards in his book *Diaghilev and the Ballets Russes* that on her summer holiday with Misia in Venice Diaghilev told Misia, with Chanel listening in silence, of his financial plight in keeping the Ballets Russes afloat with so many lavish productions. Chanel, who had attended performances of both *Le Sacre du Printemps* in 1913 and *Parade* in 1917 was enthralled by them.

28 **Portrait of Misia** *by Pierre-Auguste Renoir, 1904.*

Misia Sert, called 'a collector of geniuses' by the perceptive chronicler Paul Morand, was an influential figure in the milieu of avant-garde writers, painters, composers, and performers. In post-World War I Paris, they rapidly went up the social hierarchy. Chanel owed to Misia Sert her introduction to this new élite artistic-social world where the fashion designer won as much recognition for her creativity in the theatre as Jean Cocteau, Pablo Picasso, Igor Stravinsky and Serge Diaghilev.

Unbeknownst to Misia, Chanel gave Diaghilev a substantial cheque to carry out his projects.[4]

Besides munificent financial backing, Chanel, through Diaghilev and his circle, found herself actively working in the world of the theatre. Her first theatrical costuming was for Jean Cocteau who was at the famous dinner party of Cécile Sorel. An *esprit de corps* formed between Chanel and Cocteau, and, although their camaraderie had its ups and downs, the bond was never broken. Chanel encouraged his unconventional attitudes and also introduced him to the world of fashion. He often sketched her fashions and designed fabric motifs for her collections, in the 1930s overlapping with Elsa Schiaparelli, for whom he designed fabrics and accessories on the theme of Surrealism. Chanel's work for him had ramifications for fashion.

Chanel's first collaboration with Cocteau was for his free adaptation of Sophocles's *Antigone*. Opening night was on 20 December 1922 at the Théâtre de l'Atelier in Paris. The sets were designed by Picasso and the music was composed by Arthur Honegger. The aftermath of World War I had brought about a number of historical revivals, including classicism. In literature, Cocteau participated in this revival, in music Honegger, in art Picasso and in dress Chanel. Honegger's musical instruments consisted only of the oboe and the harp.

From 1915 Picasso was under the influence of Ingres's drawings and was executing very precise, stylized pencil drawings. By the time of *Antigone* he was well into his classical period engaged in a series of paintings and drawings based on the antique and Roman

29 **Scene of Antigone brought by two guards before King Creon.** *Greek vase painting from Lucania, c.380–370 BC.*

Chanel's costumes for the theatre and for her collections often show evident affinities with classicism. Chanel appreciated the draped, fluid, elementary forms of Greek dress. In Cocteau's play Antigone, *she clad the tragic heroine in the same style tunic.*

30 **Scene of Antigone between two guards from the play,** Antigone, *by Jean Cocteau, 1922.*

Pablo Picasso designed the sets and masks. Well into his classical period, he looked to Greek vase painting when he designed the black shields for the guards and the masks on the mantle representing children, women and old men of the Greek chorus. Chanel dressed Antigone in a long tunic-style white woollen dress edged with brown woollen bands. In the ancient Greek theatre tragic characters wore sleeved tunics reaching to the ground and decorated with coloured bands.

classicism. He looked to Greek vase paintings and masks for his motifs for *Antigone*. Chanel, whose chemise dress dated back to 1916, was also in the midst of classicism, with a Greek marble adorning her fashion house and her collections depicting flowing, classical drapery. It is interesting that Sem's poster design for Chanel No. 5 should show a *haute couture* model adoringly looking up at the bottle of perfume displaying a gesture worthy of one of Lady Emma Hamilton's 'classical attitudes' and wearing a dress having a distinctive sculptural quality to it (see **16**). In an interview Cocteau said:

> I asked Mademoiselle Chanel for the costumes because she is the greatest designer of our day and I do not see Oedipus's daughters being badly dressed.[5]

Chanel's costumes for *Antigone* elegantly recaptured the spirit of the antique past. Like Picasso she must also have looked to Greek vase painting, in particular to the scene of Antigone brought by two guards before the tyrannical King Creon (**29**). She dressed Antigone herself in a long white woollen tunic-style dress edged with brown bands (**30**). On the Greek Vase Antigone is depicted wearing a similar style of costume. Chanel must also have looked to the fashion plates of the Directoire period.

The 5 January 1800 issue of the *Journal des dames et des modes*, the leading fashion magazine of the Directoire, featured some of the last costumes of the period including a long white tunic-style dress edged with dark ribbon. Pierre de La Mésangère, the editor of the *Journal des dames et des modes*, considered this fashion plate one of the most striking examples after the antique illustrated in his periodical.[6] Over her white dress Antigone wore a loosely woven coarse woollen patterned cloak in predominantly brown tones, the whole costume in keeping with the Greek's use of wool. As Chanel herself remarked, 'Greece is wool, not silk.'[7] The material and the design also serve to enhance her dramatic gestures as the victim. All the costumes reflected proper characterization. Ismene, Antigone's sister, wore everyday dress made of wool in earth-coloured tones and King Creon a neutral-toned mantle and a gold band around his head replete with dazzling precious jewels, often considered Chanel's first piece of autograph jewellery.

Although some famous actresses as mentioned earlier had worn Chanel hats and costumes in plays, this was the first example of Chanel the theatrical costumier. Yet when the day of reckoning came and the critics pronounced on the play, it was Chanel who received all the plaudits. French *Vogue* in its number for 1 February 1923, for example, devoted an article to Cocteau's *Antigone*. Georges Lepape who in 1911 had illustrated *Les choses de Paul Poiret* was chosen by *Vogue* to do the line drawings to illustrate the article. Lavish compliments were bestowed upon Chanel.

After *Antigone* Chanel went from strength to strength. From 1924 to 1937 Chanel costumed a whole cycle of Cocteau's works. The most important one for fashion was *Le Train bleu*. With this *opérette-dansée* or 'danced operetta' directed by Serge Diaghilev and based on a play by Jean Cocteau, Chanel found herself immersed in the world of theatre and dance. *Le Train bleu* had its opening night on 20 June 1924 at the Théâtre des Champs-Elysées in Paris. The stage curtain was designed by Pablo Picasso and the sets were by the Cubist sculptor Henri Laurens. The music was composed by Darius Milhaud and the choreography by Bronislava Nijinska, sister of Nijinsky.

Picasso's stage curtain, an enlargement of his great classical painting *Two Women Running on the Beach (The Race)* of 1922, provided an ecstatic introduction to *Le Train bleu* (**31**). The painting was featured in the Tate Gallery's major Summer exhibition of 1990, *On Classic Ground: Picasso, Léger, de Chirico and the New Classicism 1910–1930*. A much neglected movement of modern art, new classicism gathered momentum during and after World War I. It was given a boost with Jean Cocteau's call for a 'return to order', entailing as it did many radical artists rejecting or modifying the revolutionary styles they themselves had developed such as Cubism and Futurism. Cocteau wanted to recreate a new

31 **Two Women Running on the Beach (The Race)** *by Pablo Picasso. The stage curtain for* Le Train bleu, *1924.*

It was an enlargement by Prince Alexandre Schervachidze to gigantic proportions, of Picasso's small gouache painted on wood. Picasso painted the women on the beach at Dinard in Brittany in the summer of 1922, where he probably saw them racing each other wearing loose, flowing classical tunics so fashionable with the cultists at the seaside who advocated a keep-fit programme.

golden age as an antidote to the physical horrors brought about by the First World War and also to the acceleration of industrialization brought about by the machine age. He was adapting classical plays such as *Antigone* discussed above and he thought artists should reject abstraction and return to human representation, in particular to the classical tradition with its emphasis on order, beauty and harmony.

Many leading avant-garde artists were commissioned to design sets and costumes for the theatre and ballet, the most celebrated being Picasso. In his stage curtain Picasso never loses sight of human values and the bursting vitality of sport. Cocteau's scenario gave balletic expression to an array of sports which were very popular among men and women in the 1920s – swimming, tennis and golf. In his interview in the Observer for 23 November 1924 Diaghilev pointed out that the costumes were by 'the greatest arbiter of fashion, Chanel.' With the theme of athleticism Chanel was the ideal fashion designer to create costumes of bathers, tennis players and golfers. Before World War I she was, as we have seen, designing and wearing sports clothes long before any of the other couturiers who became associated with sport such as Jean Patou.

A great cross-section, a veritable synthesis of modern life, partook of the hedonism on the beach in *Le Train bleu*. The character of Beau Gosse or 'Handsome Boy' was performed by the renowned

**32   Anton Dolin as Beau
Gosse and Lydia Sokolova
as Perlouse in** Le Train
bleu, *1924.*

*Chanel's bathing costumes
were very trim and hung softly
from neck to knee over bared
neck, arms, and legs.
Sokolova's bathing costume had
also lost the modesty
superfluity, the corset. Her
neat skull cap and earrings
became fashion accessories.
Sokolova also wears little
rubber bathing slippers.
Chanel's great innovation was
that she brought her own style
to the stage, designing real, not
imaginary, sportswear for the
dancers.*

classical *danseur* Anton Dolin (**32**). Cocteau's inspiration for *Le
Train bleu* was supposed to have been the artistic and technical skill
of Anton Dolin.[8] Indeed Dolin's daring high-stands and breathtaking
somersaults caused a sensation on opening night.

The role of Perlouse, the beautiful bather, was assigned to Lydia
Sokolova (see **32**). In her memoirs, *Dancing for Diaghilev*, she recalled
the fittings at Chanel's workroom in the rue Cambon.

33 **Bronislava Nijinska as the Tennis Champion, with Lydia Sokolova, in** Le Train bleu, *1924.*

Dressed in white from her headband to her tennis shoes, Nijinska's attire was modelled on that of Suzanne Lenglen, the reigning queen of tennis. The garb was practical and convenient for tennis, yet had a considerable impact on fashion.

When I tried my pink bathing-dress, which we all thought very daring, the question of what I was to wear on my head arose. Three women stood round me, binding my long hair with various pieces of material, until at last they decided on a dark suède. The neat little skull-cap they made for me set a fashion.[9]

Chanel designed some jewellery for Sokolova to wear which also entered the realm of fashion.

After the dress rehearsal of *Le Train bleu*, Mlle Chanel came to my dressing-room and said, 'I must think up some accessories for your costume'; and on the opening night I found on my dressing-table the first of the large pearl earrings which were soon to be seen everywhere. They were very smart but so heavy that they pulled at my ears and made it hard for me to hear the music. Mlle Chanel had invented a new kind of pearl, which was made of china and coated with wax. She used to wear a great many ropes of these.[10]

Originally Chanel was to have attired some of the ballerinas in fawn beach pyjamas which she had made into such a fashion success. But she changed her mind in favour of the bathing costume similar to Lydia Sokolova's. Among those in the *corps de ballet* involved in this change was Dame Ninette de Valois, who in her book *Invitation to the Dance* provides an illuminating insight into Chanel's determination not to prettify or sentimentalize but to provide the characters with real costumes and hairstyles.

Tennis was another energetic game portrayed in *Le Train bleu*. The role of Tennis Champion was performed by Bronislava Nijinska (**33**). The inspiration for this role was Suzanne Lenglen, prima donna of the tennis courts in the 1920s. Lenglen's style of dress caused as much excitement and delight as her incredible leaps which seemed to defy the laws of gravity. For she jettisoned the conventional tennis attire of long skirt, long-sleeved blouse and elaborate tie in favour of either a plain, loose-fitting knee-length white dress or a knee-length pleated white skirt worn with a sleeveless cardigan. She also dispensed with the traditional garter belt for short white stockings held in place by knee garters. What aroused the most interest for fashion was the bandeau she bound around her head. It became a fashion accessory, indeed, a hallmark of the 1920s look. Nijinska wore an all white outfit consisting of a simple, knee-length white dress, stockings, tennis shoes and of course a headband. Yet some thirteen years earlier Chanel during her equestrian jaunts around Royallieu had worn the same style headband.[11]

The part of the Golf Player in *Le Train bleu* was played by the Polish dancer, Léon Woizikovsky. For him Chanel copied the sartorial impeccability of Edward, Prince of Wales (**34**). The Prince of Wales, later King Edward VIII and Duke of Windsor, was Captain of the Royal and Ancient Golf Club of St Andrews, Fife. The painter Sir William Orpen executed an oil on canvas of the Prince dressed as Captain (**35**). The Prince made many trips to Paris during the 1920s and was an inspiration to French fashion designers, especially for his check suiting fabric. Prince of Wales check became very fashionable for womenswear, another example of the potential in

34 **Léon Woizikovsky as the Golfer, with Beau Gosse, Perlouse and the Tennis Champion in** Le Train bleu, *1924.*

The Golfer wears English-style sporting dress consisting of tweed knickerbockers or plus fours, soft-collared white cotton shirt, Fair Isle sweater, matching long socks and lace-up black shoes. Knickerbockers were a type of man's breeches but cut wider and fuller than ordinary knee breeches with the fullness overhanging the tops of the socks. They were popular for sporting and country wear since 1860. Plus fours was the term for the 1920 version of knickerbockers associated specifically with golf and so named because, to produce the requisite fullness over the knees, the length was increased by a full four inches below the knee band where it was gathered.

a male wardrobe for the modern, independent woman. Among the models Cocteau cited for his work was the Prince of Wales and Chanel 'abided by Cocteau's rules'.[12] She designed for Woizikovsky a softly-collared white shirt, knotted tie, striped sweater, tweed plus fours, striped socks, and black lace-up golf shoes. 'Perfectly smart', pronounced the Duke of Westminster, a close friend of the Prince of Wales.[13]

Chanel's costumes for *Le Train bleu* were highly elegant and aesthetic. She had a very refreshing influence on sport, especially swimming, as Diaghilev pointed out in his interview. Indeed she effected a veritable metamorphosis on the beach.

> Chanel may have been the first to display a suntan at Cannes in 1922, but surely it was her collaboration with Diaghilev on *Le Train bleu* in 1924 which started the rage. Chanel's bathing-suits became the latest thing to wear....[14]

Jean Cocteau's one-act tragedy, *Orphée*, was first performed on

35 Portrait of Edward, Prince of Wales *by Sir William Orpen, 1922.*

During the 1920s the dashing Prince of Wales promoted many fashions. This portrait shows him as Captain of the Royal and Ancient Golf Club of St Andrews, Fife. He is casually but smartly dressed in a soft-collared white shirt, tie with a geometrical pattern, Fair Isle sweater, so named after the Scottish Shetland islands where it originated, knickerbockers or plus fours and matching cap, and lace-up black shoes. Although his vestimentary elegance was specifically intended for golf, it became fashionable for informal day wear for men in the 1920s and specifically identified with the Prince of Wales.

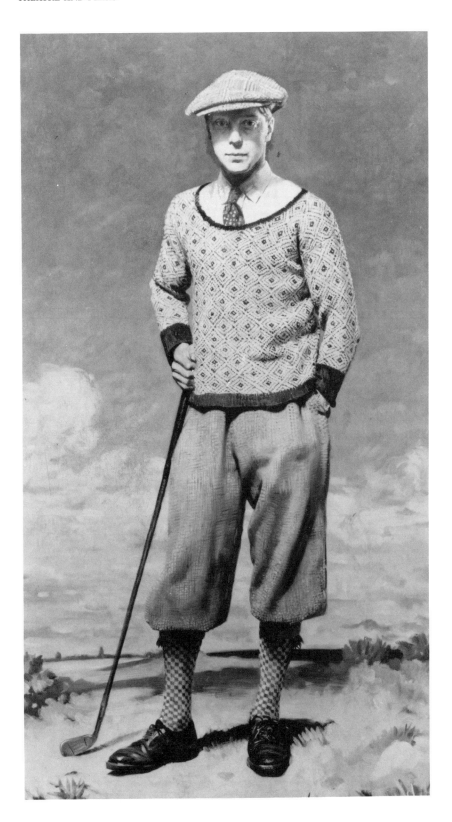

15 June 1926 at the Théâtre des Arts in Paris. It was another of Cocteau's works with an impact on fashion. This was presaged in the precise stage directions of Cocteau according to Francis Steegmuller.

> 'Clothes should be contemporary with any production. Orpheus and Eurydice should be dressed for the country, as simply and inconspicuously as possible. Death is a very beautiful young woman in a bright pink evening gown and fur coat. Coiffure, dress, coat, shoes, gestures, general deportment all up to the minute.' The simple country clothes as cut by Chanel were no less smart than her elegant evening gown, and they launched a vogue for informal dress that has 'taken us where we are today' – just as the leather jackets of the motorcyclists in the film *Orphée* were to foretell another vogue.[15]

The next work Chanel costumed was *Apollon Musagète*, a ballet by Igor Stravinsky with the collaboration of Diaghilev, premiered at the Théâtre Sarah Bernhardt in Paris on 12 June 1929. It enabled Chanel to return to her love of the dance and to work with two of her closest artistic friends. Choreography was by George Balanchine and sets and décor were by André Bauchant.

By now Chanel was not only the most celebrated fashion designer but also as the writer Maurice Sachs related:

> she in a way inaugurated the reign of couturiers. She held court, and open table and dispensed privileges and pensions.[16]

She now had a splendid town house at 29 Faubourg-Saint-Honoré, Paris, and as photographs attest she had a large library with a collection of books given her by all the leading poets and writers. Jean Hugo, the gifted painter, who had designed the sets for Cocteau's *Orphée* and who moved in Chanel's artistic and literary circles, records in his diary at this time the lavish dinner parties at Chanel's *hôtel particulier* and the brilliant writers and artists who attended them. They were always considered the highlight of every social season in Paris.[17]

HOLLYWOOD

One aspect of fashion indigenous to the 1930s is its relationship with the cinema. Films provided the perfect antidote to the economic slump of the 1930s. Mass marketing would extend to films, especially American films. Their glamorous stars in the latest fashions would provide a whole new area where women could find a way to look, and they found it most appealing.

The most famous of the movie moguls, Sam Goldwyn, thought

36 Gloria Swanson wearing a black satin bias-cut gown designed by Chanel *which she wore in the film* Tonight or Never, *1931.*

Chanel's bias-cut gowns have an easy grace and suppleness. She enjoyed using satin for her work on the bias cut because it is a material that is unstructured, elastic and has great moulding ability, creating a soft, sleek look, so beautifully exemplified by Miss Swanson.

the only way to survive the economic crisis was to attract women especially from among 'the growing number of urban rich'. His game plan: women would go to films 'one to see the pictures and the stars, and two, to see the latest clothes.'[18] His scheme was brought to fruition when he succeeded in luring Chanel to Hollywood with a lucrative contract in April 1931 to design fashions for actresses under contract to him both on and off the screen. However, the deal was short-lived. Chanel would not abandon her style nor the Hollywood goddesses theirs. The Chanel style was too simple and understated for the sensational stylizations favoured by the rebellious stars.

Nonetheless, Chanel made a good attempt at reconciliation with Gloria Swanson in the film *Tonight or Never*. The film was an adaptation of the Broadway play and won critical applause when it came out in December 1931. Gloria Swanson was then at the height of her career. Miss Swanson was not only endowed with much glamour. She also had a dynamic and lively intelligence which manifested itself in the sure touch she brought to light comedy. Her autobiography attests to her affinity with Chanel and her fashions. The fittings took place in Chanel's fashion house in

Paris. By the time of her second fitting, Miss Swanson was pregnant and had put on some weight. She came up against the steely determination and perfectionism of Chanel for her craft.

> The following day Coco Chanel, tiny and fierce, approaching fifty, wearing a hat as she always did at work, glared furiously at me when I had trouble squeezing into one of the gowns she had measured for me six weeks earlier. It was black satin to the floor, cut on the bias, a great work of art in the eyes of both of us. I said I would try it on with a girdle, but when I stepped before her again, she snorted with contempt and said anyone a block away could see the line where the girdle ended halfway down my thigh.
> 'Take off the girdle and lose five pounds,' she snapped briskly.[19]

Gloria Swanson's classic looks and svelte figure admirably suited the Chanel style (**36**). Chanel moulded the satin in the round giving Miss Swanson's gown a fluid simplicity, indeed, a twentieth-century Grecian silhouette. It is an excellent example of Chanel the technician. Both the Grand Duchess Marie Pavlovna and Colette have left vivid portraits of Chanel at work describing the methods she used to create a design such as the gown in this film. The Grand Duchess has written that

> for several years I watched Chanel's creative genius express itself through her fingers. She never designed anything on paper and would make a dress either according to an idea in her head or as she proceeded....Bonjour Jeanne. This was the only moment when Chanel would look up at the model's face; the rest of the time she would be entirely concentrated on the figure....Then the fitting began, a slow and careful procedure.[20]

These fittings of *la pose* as Colette called them could last anything up to seven or eight hours during which time Mademoiselle, as Chanel had always to be addressed, did everything from pinning to snipping, from pinching to pulling, ultimately falling to her knees and sitting back on her legs 'like a washerwoman' all in order to fashion the garment to her exacting and impeccable taste. The end result of such fierce and total concentration on the draped model, to whom she often had to hiss to keep still, was that Chanel clothes were always comfortable.

Chanel also dressed Miss Swanson in one of her classic suits for one of the scenes in *Tonight or Never* (**37**). Not surprisingly Chanel also had one of the same suits and was often photographed in it. It epitomizes her style of the 1930s when she perfected much of the tailoring with regard to fit and cut. The jacket is cut shorter and is shaped to the waist. Chanel herself emphasized this by wearing a very wide leather belt. The suit has wide revers and is given definition by the collar of the immaculate white blouse. Chanel had a veritable love affair with the white blouse with its purity of colour and austere cut, so much a part of her pared-down dressing.

Although her time in Hollywood was not a wild success and she was released from her contract by Sam Goldwyn, her peregrinations in the New World were the way in which Chanel observed the fashion scene of New York and met heads of department stores and fashion editors of magazines, which was invaluable for publicizing and marketing her fashions. Chanel returned to Paris and in the period 1934–7 she resumed working for Jean Cocteau who by now was the most influential figure in the theatre. Chanel created the costumes for three more of his plays. For *Les Chevaliers de la table ronde*, inspired by the myth of the Holy Grail, she had the assistance of Christian Dior. Her flair for theatrical costuming was so instinctive that she could immediately pinpoint any muddling on the part of Cocteau, as, for example, in *La Machine infernale*.[21] Her most controversial work of all was for Cocteau's adaptation of Sophocles's *Oedipe roi* where she designed subtle wrappings of narrow strips of cloth which the critics deemed scandalous. She also costumed two French films, *La Marseillaise* in 1938 and *La Règle du jeu* in 1939, both directed by Jean Renoir.

On the eve of World War II Chanel formed a friendship with Salvador Dali. This surprised many as he also developed a great friendship with her only rival throughout the 1930s, Elsa Schiaparelli. In spite of her many artistic friendships Chanel did not collect paintings unlike Jacques Doucet and Paul Poiret. She claimed her eyesight was too bad to permit her to appreciate them and she preferred to collect and read books, many of them given her, as mentioned above, by some of the most distinguished poets and writers in Paris. Yet it is significant that in her apartment there was one small oil canvas depicting a sheaf of wheat, the symbol of life itself, and it was by Salvador Dali.

In 1939 Dali composed for the Ballets Russes of Monte Carlo a ballet entitled *Bacchanale*. He was inspired by the life of King Ludwig II of Bavaria, the 'Dream King' who preferred the role of actor to kingship, playing out his life on a permanent stage set without an audience but with changing scenery based on the operas of Richard Wagner. Dali chose Chanel to design the costumes and she lavishly responded to the fantasy world of this nineteenth-century monarch. Their splendour recreated not only the complicated dreams and desires of the Mad King but also perhaps reflected a sense of escapism on the eve of World War II. In his autobiography Dali gives this vivid description of the costumes:

I also had the good fortune to have Chanel take upon herself the designing of the costumes. Chanel worked with a wholehearted enthusiasm and created the most luxurious costumes that have ever been conceived for the theatre. She used real ermine, real jewels and the gloves of Ludwig II of Bavaria were so heavily embroidered that we felt some anxiety as to whether the dancer would be able to dance with them on.[22]

Dali noted in his autobiography that they were kindred spirits although their creativity was different. In August 1939 Dali and his wife were staying near Bordeaux where Chanel visited them.

Her originality was the opposite of mine. I have always either shamelessly 'exhibited' my ideas, or else hidden them with a refined Jesuitical hypocrisy. Not she: she does not exhibit them, nor does she hide them. She dresses them. The sense of clothes had in her a biological significance of self-modesty of a mortal and fatal violence. What Ludwig II of Bavaria dresses Chanel must have designed 'to dress', for formal occasions and for street-wear, the young and hard bitterness of her unavowed sentiments! Her sense of fashion and of costume was 'tragic' – as in others it is 'cynical'. Above all Chanel was the being possessing the best dressed 'body and soul' on earth.[23]

37 Gloria Swanson wearing a Chanel suit *in* Tonight or Never, *1931.*

The disciplined, restrained and elegant Chanel suit of the 1930s, showing the alterations made with regard to cut and fit. Its simplicity and clarity and clean, contemporary edge is echoed in the white blouse.

Throughout this chapter it is evident from contemporary accounts that Chanel was held in high esteem by artists and writers.

Today some fashion writers who criticize Chanel have little understanding of this esteem and admiration. Comments have been made misconstruing the remarks of those in her circle.

> Despite her reputation for chic, Chanel was essentially unsophisticated, hard-headed and ruthless. She was a primitive in the artistic circles in which she moved; Colette described her as a 'little black bull'.[24]

If one carefully reads the entire passage in context in Colette's *Prisons et paradis*, the portrait she evokes of Chanel is quite different from the above description. As Jean Leymarie so sagaciously points out:

> She admired Chanel's willpower and her concern for perfection in her craft. By her stubborn energy, her way of facing things, of listening, the defensiveness which barricades her face sometimes, Chanel is a black bull. A dark, curly lock of hair falls over her forehead, down to her eyebrows, and dances with each movement of her head, like a young bull's forelock. Work is the secret behind her intense conqueror's mien.[25]

Colette was also a journalist who wrote fashion reviews and therefore appreciated Chanel's exacting standards and total absorption in her work. And the source from which this emanated? 'It was the artists who taught me exactness.'[26] Colette and Chanel also had another affinity in their admiration of craftsmen and love for the handmade, another link with artists. Whether for her fashions or for her theatrical costuming Chanel's total immersion, passionate zeal and exactitude were the same.

Chanel herself was eulogized by the theatre in the Broadway musical, *Coco*, based on her life, with the equally indefatigable Katharine Hepburn in the starring role. Directed by Alan Jay Lerner the play featured some two hundred and fifty costumes designed by Sir Cecil Beaton.

Writers and artists were Chanel's friends and mentors. She earned their admiration and respect both near and far. When George Bernard Shaw was asked to name the two most influential women of the twentieth century, he unhesitatingly answered 'Curie and Chanel.'[27]

4 COMEBACK

Various reasons are given for the astonishing comeback of Chanel at the age of seventy-one, after a fifteen year gap in her career. *Vogue*'s Bettina Ballard maintained that

> Chanel didn't re-open in 1954 to worry about a successful couture business; she went back to designing to escape boredom and to keep young.[1]

However, Chanel was astute both as a *couturière* and as a *femme d'entreprise*. More convincing motives are advanced by Iris Ashley, a British fashion writer and columnist at the time. Chanel's bold gesture had partly to do with the sales of her perfumes which

> in America were falling off, and her financial advisers were of the opinion that a successful re-opening of her *salons de couture* would give the perfume sales a new boost.[2]

PARIS RE-VISITED: CHANEL VERSUS THE MALE FASHION DESIGNERS

The other and far more telling reason was the dominance of male fashion designers, in particular Christian Dior.

> Dior's New Look had evolved into an hour-glass silhouette, or figure of eight....
> There was even a small waist-corset (invented by Jacques Fath) called a *guêpière*, which was known evocatively in English as a 'waspie'. This was luckily only worn with evening dresses, for it pulled in the waist to such an extent that it was a choice between not eating, or suffering from acute indigestion until it was possible to retire and undress. Mademoiselle Chanel is reported to have

remarked that such a pulled-in waistline was '... an exaggeration, even on a wasp'.[3]

Chanel was always on the side of women. She wanted *haute couture* to be comfortable which she didn't think was the case when it was designed by men. Furthermore, a male fashion designer like Dior couldn't possibly have the best interests of women in mind when his New Look made them look grand and stately. She, on the other hand, had made them look young and would do so again. Although now seventy-one she still had the figure of a *jeune fille*. So when Chanel announced to the world that on Friday, 5 February 1954 she was unveiling her first collection since the onset of World War II she was in effect giving a contemptuous retort to Dior and the other male fashion designers. Iris Ashley attended the big event.

> ... I thought Mademoiselle Chanel had started another revolution of fashion. Just how she put it across was hard to define in writing. The clothes were so undramatic.
>
> The shapes were all the same: the neat collarless cardigan-style jackets, the slightly flared skirts falling from a small but not overly-tight waistband, the pretty blouses, with the soft 'pussy-cat' bows. It was chiefly the colours, the fabrics, the sheer feminine softness of outline, that made you realize how hard and forced the silhouette of fashion had become.[4]

Karl Lagerfeld, then a young apprentice at the Chambre Syndicale de la Couture Parisienne said he 'loved this look that harked back to a pre-war world I hadn't known but found more intoxicating than any current fashion'[5]

One of the people most instrumental in promoting Chanel's comeback was Bettina Ballard.

> I photographed three full pages of Chanel models and *Vogue* backed up my fashion judgement by opening the March issue with them. The frontispiece showed Marie-Hélène Arnaud, a completely unknown mannequin, whom Chanel had created in her own image, leaning against the wall in a navy jersey suit with her hands plunged deep in her pockets, her tucked white lawn blouse buttoned onto the easy skirt under her loose open jacket, her navy cuffs rolled back to show the white ones, and a navy straw sailor hat with ribbon streamers on the back of her head. I had owned practically the identical suit before the war ....[6]

Indeed, if a Chanel suit from the 1930s is placed beside one from the 1950s there is remarkably little difference between them. Although spanning some forty years in date, her costumes from the 1950s could again easily be worn in 1990 and it is the simple

38 **Three Chanel costumes.**

Right to left: *Ensemble consisting of a dress of silk chiffon printed in cerise, orange and black with a coat of yellow and grey wool tweed lined in the dress fabric, c.1927; suit of blue linen with the distinctive Chanel touch, the flower on the jacket, 1937; suit of black, blue and azure tweed, c.1955; all labelled Chanel. They exemplify Chanel's maxim: 'Always remove, never put back, no button without its button hole – the underside as perfect as the outside.'*

The collar and cuffs of the coat, for example, have no facings. Chanel had the raw edges turned over and stitched with machine stitching, a decorative feature seen also on the body of the coat. The selvedge edge was used on the coat's centre fronts. The lining of the coat matches the dress and was meticulously hand-stitched so that the stitches cannot be seen on the outside. The raw edges of the jacket of the suit on the right are again just turned over and machine-stitched.

line and expert craftsmanship that make them so modern (**38**).

Bettina Ballard said how much she had missed these comfortable, reliable young clothes and was sure other women would want them too, if they saw them. When she returned to New York she was determined to continue to sound the bugles for Chanel.

By the time of her next collection classic chic had regained its pre-eminence. A great many of the buyers and press had all of a sudden 'rediscovered' Chanel and in a very few months the 'Chanel look' was a best seller.[7] It was the Chanel suit in particular that had regained its ascendency not only in *haute couture* but also in ready-to-wear, being widely copied in the United States and Europe by firms such as Saks Fifth Avenue in New York and Geoffrey Wallis in London. She took particular pride in being copied – *les trouvailles sont faites pour être perdues.* Although she continued to maintain her firm belief that while 'I like fashion to go down into the street, but I can't accept that it should originate there'[8] there was no doubt that she could easily fit in. The ready-to-wear industry by the 1950s was a very fast-growing one. Recognition that conditions had changed since Chanel closed her house during World War II was manifested by the development of a ready-to-wear line by the major *maisons de couture.*

The year 1949 saw the birth of ready-to-wear styles and fashion houses had to adapt to a vastly expanded clientele, and this required

39 Chanel suit, 1964.

Made in tweed with a chain-weighted jacket, the famous Chanel suit is as fashionable today as it was in the 1960s. Worn with her definitive sartorial accessories the two-toned sling-back shoes, flesh-coloured stockings and hat. One of Chanel's most famous maxims was 'A woman's education consists of two lessons: never to leave the house without stockings, never to go out without a hat'.

a standardization both modern and classical of styles which Chanel felt capable of mastering because of her unerring feminine taste and unfailing craftsmanship.[9]

SIMPLICITY AND ELEGANCE CONTINUED

Her staple outfit, the tailored suit, Chanel now updated, but she never departed from the sartorial principles she devised so long ago. The suit was made of tweed, wool, jersey, silk – the material governed by whether the suit would be worn for day wear or evening wear. The jacket was invariably short and fitted, decorated with pockets and fastened with gold buttons. The suit was meticulously lined with silk in a toning colour, being a decorative effect in itself. If a blouse was worn with the suit, it matched the lining in material and colour. The skirt skimmed the knee as this was the part of the anatomy Chanel found unflattering. Gilt chains, pearl earrings, two-tone pumps, stockings of a shade which merged imperceptibly with the shoes, a quilted handbag with gilt chains and a hat, flat bow or gardenia in the hair all gave a soft, feminine effect. Every feature was special and individual to Chanel and what made the ensemble classic. (Colour Plates 7 and 9). The jacket and skirt produce a flawless line. The understated elegance of a Chanel suit is as carefully made inside as outside. A gold chain is always used for weighting along the lower inside edge of the jacket. This makes the whole line of the suit very straight with not a bit of clutter or fussiness and when the model moved the jacket would not ride up.

Another distinguishing attribute of a Chanel *haute couture* suit that is not found in ready-to-wear is that her pure silk linings have tucks in areas such as the shoulders, all the stitching done by hand, which means the suit can take a great deal of stress after continuous wear. In ready-to-wear darts are used which cannot bear the strain and invariably break open. But the secret of the Chanel suit is the armholes. In dressmaking generally the armhole is a very significant part of the garment. If the sleeves fit badly the whole ensemble can be ruined. When the fit is imperfect the fault can usually be found at the armholes. Chanel pulled open the armholes of her suits time and again in order to get a closer fit. If a Chanel suit is examined carefully it will be noticed that the armhole is small and high, which, as a result gives the wearer a graceful long neck and fragile shoulders, enhancing femininity.

In keeping with her depth of knowledge about fabrics, and instinctive flair for using them, Chanel in 1966 designed a suit in the unusual material, silk *cloqué* (**40**). Derived from the French word for blistered, *cloqué* denoted a fabric with a raised and irregular

40 Ivory-textured silk cloqué suit, 1966.

Although this suit bears no label it has all the characteristics associated with Chanel: the interlocking Cs on the buttons, the influence of her sportswear in the easy, blazer-like cut of the jacket, the detailed stitching and the gold chain found inside the jacket to weigh down the edges and produce the impeccable line found only in Chanel suits.

surface. The collar of the jacket is small and turned down and
stitched in rows of floss silk, a decorative device that gives the suit
a fine, light, downy touch. The skirt has a crossover front and inset
waistband. Chanel would not have approved of the short skirt, as
she always cited the knees as unsightly. However, this was the
period of the mini-skirt, a style, needless to say, Chanel hated!

Many of Chanel's suits show a stylish sense of colour that would
have made Renoir envious. A few examples: about 1960 she
designed a suit of pink angora wool twill with a multi-coloured
chiné-printed silk taffeta blouse (Colour Plate 7). In 1968 a mohair
and tweed suit was printed in green, orange and turquoise on an

ivory ground (Colour Plate 9). The colours are bright and the patterns lack a firm outline which combined achieve a naturalism that animates the suits.

Issues of *Vogue* from the time of Chanel's comeback show that women who wore high quality fashion design had a very structured lifestyle with clothes appropriate to every occasion just as before World War II.

One of the most popular fashionable occasions was the cocktail party which usually began around 6 p.m. A Chanel tailored suit such as the one made in *cloqué* would have been eminently suitable. Chanel also designed some charming short evening dresses for which great attention would have been paid to Chanel accessories to complete the ensemble (**41**). Although having a fitted waist, the fluid, less-structured Chanel line has returned to evening fashions in marked contrast to the Dior and Balenciaga evening styles.

After her return in 1954 Chanel developed her little black dress. One example, dated *c*.1960, and labelled Chanel, is made of a combination of black chiffon and black satin ribbon (**42**). Unlike her pre-war film clientele, actresses now clamoured to wear Chanel fashions. They not only wore her creations in films but were also featured in the fashion press. Chanel was sought after by the *nouvelle vague* directors and she designed the costumes for many of their films. In 1961 Delphine Seyrig starred in *Last Year at Marienbad* directed by Alain Resnais. She wore a little black dress not dissimilar in style to the one discussed above, being made in black crêpe and decorated with small, pleated muslin frills. These little black dresses have a mystique, an almost dreamy quality about them, perfect for the haunting quality of the *nouvelle vague* films. The enduring popularity of Chanel's post-war little black dress is attested to by the fact that leading fashion designers still include it in their collections.

Oriental influences, seen in the work of Chanel early on in her career, surfaced again during her comeback. About 1959 she designed an evening gown, which would have come under *Vogue*'s heading as suitable for 'benefits and balls' (Colour Plate 6). The evening gown is made of black silk embossed with gold lamé, a favourite Chinese combination. It is a Chanel evening gown of rich embellishment and simple lines. Lamé became a favourite material of Chanel's after her comeback.

In 1962 she designed the costumes for the actress Romy Schneider to wear in Luchino Visconti's film, *Boccaccio 70*. One of the most impressive outfits was a gold lamé tunic dress, very refined and with a sunburst tonality akin to Chinese robes. Around this same date Chanel continued the theme with a tunic-coat and skirt thus making the tunic as fashionable in the 1960s as Poiret had

41 **Organza and silk cocktail dress designed by Chanel, c.1958.**

Opposite left: *This zestful dress has a blue and white striped silk boned corsage, with a large matching bow. The organza skirt, worn over stiffened petticoats, has a blue and white striped silk band to trim the hem. The nautical palette of striped navy and white creates a light and airy feeling, enhanced by using the sheer fabric, organza, for the skirt.*

42 **Little black dress designed by Chanel, c.1960.**

Opposite right: *A fine example of that mainstay of the Chanel wardrobe designed during her comeback. It is made of quality materials, chiffon and satin and has a flattering cut. Emphasis is placed on the body in movement with the deep satin ribbon waistband setting off the pleated chiffon bodice, hips and flared skirt. Chanel's logicality and minimalism creates a beauty of line and balance.*

43 Trouser suit in green and red printed gauze brocaded in gold, designed by Chanel, c.1970.

Chanel's evocation of chinoiserie in fabric and design has an elegant informality. Her comeback trouser suits in this style were intended for private evening gatherings.

44 Black worsted crêpe dress and jacket and black silk stockinet hat, designed by Chanel, mid-1960s.

Chanel made this schoolgirl-like outfit for herself. It is the acme of her minimalist approach, for the ensemble is totally functional, the components pared down to the bare essentials. Decoration is provided by the white blouse and the costume jewellery.

in the early part of the century. During her comeback Chanel designed some trouser suits: the most aesthetic showed Chinese influences. One very splendid example, dating from *c.*1970, is made in green and red printed gauze brocaded in gold (**43**). The jacket is in the mandarin style, straight, loose, with a small standing collar and worn with tubular-cut trousers.

One of the most pervasive art movements to emerge in the 1960s was Minimalism, an uncompromising and rigorous aesthetic that was noted for its simplified geometric abstraction. Chanel showed what an uncompromising and rigorous fashion designer she was by creating for herself in the 1960s a very austere two-piece outfit (**44**). A fashion formula dating back to her pre-war period, it is here repeated and reinterpreted, imbued with modernity. For it is a costume totally stark, stripped down to its bare essentials echoing Minimal art of the mid-1960s. The features of Minimal Art could be said to be those of Chanel's outfit: sculptural, simple, and having a unitary form. It is also the ultimate example of Chanel as her own best advertisement for it was in the sale of her personal wardrobe sold at Christie's London in 1978. The sale catalogue points out how she wore this very streamlined outfit many times in Switzerland and in Italy including at a gala film première of her great friend, the celebrated director Luchino Visconti.[10] Her sale

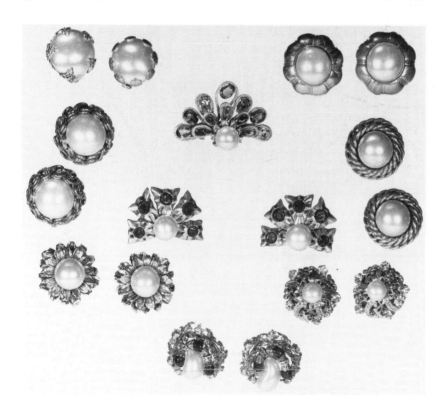

45 An essential ingredient of Chanel's style was her costume jewellery. *Pre-eminence was given to pearls.*

Highlights among the interesting examples shown here from Chanel's personal collection are: a pair of simulated pearl earrings with gilt mounts formed as a double chain mount; a pair of gilt metal earrings in the form of flowers with simulated pearl centres; a single earring or clip formed as half a daisy of gilt metal set with a pearl, amber, yellow, purple and white paste; a pair of fan-shaped gilt earrings set with pearls and red paste; and a pair of simulated pearl earrings with gilt mounts formed as a double rope.

46   Brooches were another of Chanel's favourite costume jewels which complemented the masterful simplicity of her clothes and provided the perfect finishing touch.

Top row: *a brooch of curved lozenge-shape set with three large and five smaller simulated emerald stones; a brooch of lozenge-shape, the pierced gilt metal mount set with a simulated cabochon emerald and paste.*

Bottom row: *a brooch comprising a square simulated emerald in a circular gilt metal mount repoussé with rocaille and set with paste and having three baroque pearls suspended below; a bar-brooch of red, blue and green paste.*

47   Two tubular bangles.

The one on the left has gilt-metal scales, set with a central artificial pearl in Renaissance mount flanked by two red glass beads with simulated acorn finials. The one on the right is set with a simulated cabochon emerald in the centre. These bracelets are unique. They were the last of Chanel's jewellery designs, shortly before her death, and were never put into production.

included only one long evening gown for it 'was not Mademoiselle's habit to change in the evening. She wore the same suit all day long changing only her scarves and jewellery.'[11] For this ensemble pearls reign supreme, her pearls figuring very prominently in the sale of her casket of costume jewellery (**45**). Jewelled brooches often adorned her hats as this costume shows and again numerous examples dating from her comeback were sold in the Christie's sale (**46**). The highlight of the sale were some pieces that are unique, being designed shortly before Chanel's death and never put into production (**47**).

Cecil Beaton with his usual flair for characterization and reflection wrote in *The Glass of Fashion*, that

> ...the designer must have the absolute and authoritative genius to impose his or her vision of the needs of the times on the times themselves, so that fashions which a year previously would have been considered outrageous are suddenly a necessity. It is the genius who creates the need, though that need must reflect the unconscious wishes of the moment if the genius is to be accepted, at least by his contemporaries.[12]

It is not surprising that the icon herself refused to go to London in 1963 to receive the award of Fashion Immortal from the *Sunday Times* for the same reason that she refused the *Légion d'Honneur* before World War II – it had been given to other fashion designers. But she did travel to Dallas, Texas in 1957 to receive the Neiman-Marcus Award for the fashion designer who had the most significant influence on twentieth-century fashion.

CONCLUSION

THE HOUSE OF CHANEL

Following the death of Chanel in 1971 the task of carrying on her tradition was bestowed upon Gaston Berthelot who came from Christian Dior, New York. Although he managed several seasons of collections, it was a hard act to follow the peerless Coco. A new perfume, Cristalle, came on the market in 1974. However, the real revitalization of the House of Chanel came in 1977 with the establishment of the ready-to-wear collection. Philippe Guibourgé, who had trained under Jacques Fath and who had had a long period at Christian Dior, Paris, was appointed director of Chanel ready-to-wear. Guibourgé's instructions were to keep the Chanel style as easy and as youthful as Mademoiselle had and also to keep it up-to-date. That he did this successfully is exemplified by the fact that

> within a year there were nineteen boutiques in major cities stretching across the USA from coast to coast and from north to south, as well as in Canada. Europe followed suit as boutiques were opened in Belgium, Germany, Switzerland and France. Then came the Far East with Hong Kong and Japan. Last year, as part of a Chanel festival, a boutique was opened on the ground floor of the House of Chanel as well.[1]

Guibourgé's ready-to-wear collection dressed Chanel's devoted admirers world-wide, including London, where a boutique was also opened. The *haute couture* side of the enterprise was managed from 1974 by two fashion designers closely associated with Coco, Jean Cazaubon and Yvonne Dudel. In 1980 the Basque-born Ramone Esparza was added to the list of fashion designers who worked for the House of Chanel.

A new lease of life was given to the House of Chanel in 1983 with the appointment of Karl Lagerfeld as design director for both the *haute couture* and ready-to-wear lines. By 1985 he had made the back-to-back linked double C logo the most enviable and the most copied brand label. Lagerfeld was born in Hamburg, Germany. At the age of fourteen, he was sent to study in Paris. Within a couple of years he had won the International Wool Secretariat's fashion competition. He went to work first for Pierre Balmain followed by the House of Patou. His most distinctive work has been for Fendi where he designed some adventurous and colourful fur coats and jackets and for Chloé where he presented his ready-to-wear garments with great éclat. Given his background and the fact that Coco mistrusted male fashion designers, all this heightened by the way he proceeds, by means of drawings, whereas Mademoiselle shaped her clothes on the live model, Lagerfeld was a surprising choice for the House of Chanel. Even his first *haute couture* collection was labelled 'Chanel' not 'Karl Lagerfeld for Chanel'. However, what Bettina Ballard said of Chanel herself could equally apply to Lagerfeld.

> She is a maverick in the couture world, going her own way for her own entertainment, pursuing her own beliefs.[2]

KARL LAGERFELD: INNOVATOR WITH FLAIR AND STYLE

Lagerfeld himself has said: 'I want to make the clothes more graphic, more fun, but distinguished by touches that change slightly from one season to the next.'[3] Lagerfeld transposes the themes much as Coco did herself. It is fitting that a new perfume, aptly named Coco, came out in 1984, so soon after the start of his reign. With his prodigious talent and imagination he is brilliantly carrying on her legacy for he goes back to her roots for each of his collections but also moves with the times.

An example of this is Lagerfeld's exquisite wool bouclé and wool jersey day ensemble consisting of a dress and jacket from his Autumn/Winter 1987 collection which the House of Chanel has given to the Victoria and Albert Museum. Lagerfeld has retained the classic chic of the Chanel suit with its cardigan style, collarless jacket finished with gilt buttons and gold weighted chain, worn with a fitted short-sleeved dress. The combination of the striped wool bouclé and plain wool jersey recalls the soft tweeds and braided trimmings of Chanel's earlier styles, while Lagerfeld has also introduced the contemporary wide shoulders and short, tight skirt.

Lagerfeld has produced that very sharp, beautifully proportioned and supple silhouette that the original progenitor would have admired. And the house model appointed in 1984, Inès de la Fressange was the reincarnation of Coco herself with her elegant, dark good looks and tall, boyish figure, with even the same vivacious personality so full of intelligence and wit at the shows (Colour Plate 9). It was her image in the likeness of Coco that provided the inspiration for Lagerfeld and raised the House of Chanel to new, dizzying heights after a time when it had become rather moribund. The modern Chanel woman was the result of an interaction between fashion designer and muse.

> The new Chanel image developed from their joint perceptions of the Grande Mademoiselle herself. 'It was her personality, much more than her clothes, or the models of the time like Suzy Parker, which gave the house its image', says Inès.[4]

As with Coco Chanel herself, the creative imagination of Karl Lagerfeld has included some ventures into historicism. Like the dominatrix of twentieth-century fashion, the master has most poignantly and elegantly captured the spirit of Watteau. His Spring/Summer 1985 collection saw a superb interpretation of both the celebrated Watteau sackback dress with his evening ensemble of gown and Watteau back-pleated coat and his evening trouser suit with its evocation of Watteau's *Pierrot (Gilles)*.

Who are the customers who can afford the *haute couture* costumes described above? There are some striking parallels with Coco Chanel's clients. Today they are called the 'Shiny Set' and their yearly whirl of social activities as described by Nicolas Coleridge in his fascinating book *The Fashion Conspiracy* hardly differs from that of the *beau monde* of the 1920s and 1930s. According to figures compiled by the Chambre Syndicale de la Couture Parisienne, there are about 3,000 women world-wide who can afford *haute couture*.[5]

Are not Lagerfeld's *haute couture* designs, especially his ventures into historicism, art works of tomorrow? The exhibitions and sales of *haute couture* undertaken by Spink and Son in London in 1989–90 and Néret-Minet and Coutau-Bégarie in Paris in 1990, where the work of Coco Chanel, especially her impressive evening wear, was one of the star attractions, show the world-wide interest in the costumes of Chanel as art historical objects amongst collectors.

The parting of the fashion designer and his model-muse came in 1989 when Inès de la Fressange agreed to become the model for the new Marianne. It will be remembered that Paul Iribe drew Coco Chanel's likeness for his cover design of Marianne that adorned *Le Témoin* in 1934. Chosen as the new couture model was Claudia Schiffer, the antithesis of Inès and Coco. German, with blonde

48 **Outfit for Chanel** *by Karl Lagerfeld.*

Traditional Chanel details live on in this ensemble from the Spring/Summer Collection of 1987.

tousled hair and an hour-glass figure, she is more akin to the young Brigitte Bardot. The January 1990 show revealed that Claudia also has a bouncy, springy gait as opposed to the shoulders-back, hips-thrust-forward stance of Inès that originated with Coco and her models. To Lagerfeld, Claudia epitomizes the look of the 1990s.

His Chanel style for the 1990s requires not a boyish figure, but a womanly one. Every stitch of this collection was on the curve and the hourglass cut of the jackets – arc seaming at the bosom and straight panels at the back – was masterful.[6]

To go with these elongated curvy, tailored jackets Lagerfeld designed some very short skirts in pale chiffon. Lagerfeld's explanation:

It all began with the legs. I made skirts flesh-coloured so the legs would float in a cloud.[7]

The airy, floating movement was enhanced by the use of bright, summery colours for the jackets, such as pink and Kelly green. Lagerfeld even jettisoned the skirt altogether turning the long-line jacket into a coatdress. For his *haute couture* customers Lagerfeld seems to be responding to demand with abbreviated skirts, for very short dresses appear even at the most grand of galas. The playing around with hemlines, achieving a slim silhouette with a very long jacket worn over either a short skirt, leggings or long boots, is a Lagerfeld original. And the *homage à Coco* is there. By couture week July 1990 Lagerfeld offered a boxy jacket tucked in at the top by sloped shoulders made in the familiar bouclés and tweeds. Lagerfeld cleverly paid respect to Mademoiselle's legendary dislike of the knees by producing thigh-high boots to match the short wool and tweed suits and the satin and velvet evening gowns slashed to mid-thigh.

Lagerfeld has continued his 'floating tailoring' idea with his 1990–91 collections (Colour Plate 12). Jackets, he believed, should define the body not suppress it. His streamlined and waisted tweed suits were worn over leggings, his lightweight black body-wrap dresses were worn over black bodysuits, and bolero jackets and high-waisted skirts that Coco loved so much were worn over long-sleeved T-shirts. The mood was loose and easy on top and tight underneath. Lagerfeld's perception is that his leggings and ribbed tights are the trousers of the 1990s.

Lagerfeld's sheer effervescence and unbridled imagination has produced delightful and witty designs. He does nevertheless take his inspiration from the Chanel past. His recent first cruise-wear line is a testament to that. But surely the classic chic Chanel cardigan worn over 'flexible stretch' leggings or bodysuit is just as much in the elegant, easy, comfortable style originated by Coco. The Chanel woman has been launched into the modern sportswear sphere of the 1990s. During the reign of Coco it would have been difficult for any woman who wanted to look young and modern to go wrong with her fashions. The same can be said of Karl Lagerfeld for Chanel today. Clothes with the Chanel imprimatur no doubt will remain just as fashionable into the twenty-first century.

NOTES TO THE TEXT

Introduction

1 C. Beaton, *The Glass of Fashion*, Cassell, facsimile edition, 1989, p. 161.
2 E. Charles-Roux, *Chanel*, trs. N. Amphoux, Collins Harvill, 1989, p. 208.
3 M. Haedrich, *Coco Chanel. Her Life, Her Secrets*, trs. C.L. Markmann, Robert Hale & Co., 1972, p. 18.
4 J. Leymarie, *Chanel*, Editions d'Art Albert Skira, 1987, p. 7.
5 Marie, Grand Duchess of Russia, *A Princess in Exile*, Cassell, 1932, pp. 159–60.
6 M. Ginsburg, *Paris Fashions. The Art Deco Style of the 1920s*, Bracken Books, 1989, p. 16.
7 Charles-Roux, *op. cit.*, p. 246.
8 *Ibid.*, p. xvii.
9 Leymarie, *op. cit.*, p. 167.
10 Charles-Roux, *op. cit.*, p. 252.
11 Leymarie, *op. cit.*, p. 218.
12 Charles-Roux, *op. cit.*, p. 368.
13 Fine Arts Museums of San Francisco, *New Look to Now*, Rizzoli, 1989, p. 46.
14 Christie's London, *The Chanel Wardrobe and Casket of Costume Jewellery*, Sale of the Personal Collection of Chanel, 2 December 1978, unpaginated.
15 B. Ballard, *In My Fashion*, Secker & Warburg, 1960, p. 63.

Chapter 1

1 A. Mackrell, *Paul Poiret*, Batsford, 1990, Chapter 4. For excellent entries on Poiret in sales catalogues see Sotheby's Monaco, *Mode des Années 1840–1970. Collection Mary Vaudoyer*, 1987 and Spink and Son, London, *Haute Couture at Spink. An Illustrated Catalogue of Costume for Sale from Our Collection of Haute Couture*, 1989.
2 Arts Council of Great Britain, *Raoul Dufy 1877–1953*, London, 1983, p. 38; E. Wilson and L. Taylor, *Through the Looking Glass. A History of Dress from 1860 to the Present Day*, BBC Books, 1989, p. 87; respectively.
3 E. Carter, *Magic Names of Fashion*, Weidenfeld & Nicolson, 1980, p. 57.
4 Charles-Roux, *op. cit.*, p. 63.
5 *Ibid.*, p. 69.
6 Leymarie, *op. cit.*, p. 47.
7 A. Mackrell, *The Dress of the Parisian Élégantes with Special Reference to the Journal des Dames et des Modes from June 1797 until December 1799*, unpublished M.A. thesis, Courtauld Institute of Art, London, 1977, pp. 39–41.
8 Charles-Roux, *op. cit.*, pp. 139–40.
9 *Ibid.*, pp. 147–8.
10 *Ibid.*, p. 155.
11 Leymarie, *op. cit.*, p. 57.
12 British *Vogue*, Early August 1919, p. 28.
13 G. Howell, *In Vogue*, Penguin Books, 1978, p. 31.
14 *Ibid.*, p. 45.
15 Charles-Roux, *Chanel and Her World*, Weidenfeld & Nicolson, 1982, p. 195.
16 C. Evans and M. Thornton, *Women and Fashion. A New Look*, Quartet Books, 1989, pp. 122–32.
17 Leymarie, *op. cit.*, p. 132.
18 *Ibid.*, p. 135.
19 Charles-Roux, *Chanel and Her World*, *op. cit.*, p. 157.
20 C. Baillén, *Chanel Solitaire*, trs. B. Bray, Collins, 1973, p. 69.
21 F. Kennett, *Coco. The Life and Loves of Gabrielle Chanel*, Victor Gollancz, 1989, p. 74.
22 Wilson and Taylor, *op. cit.*, pp. 88–9.
23 A. Latour, *Kings of Fashion*, trs. M. Savill, Weidenfeld & Nicolson, 1958, p. 192.

24 Charles-Roux, *Chanel, op. cit.*, pp. 53, 184, 204, 223–4; Beaton, *op. cit.*, p. 166; Kennett, *op. cit.*, p. 10.
25 Leymarie, *op. cit.*, p. 122.
26 J. Mulvagh, *Costume Jewelry in Vogue*, Thames & Hudson, 1988, p. 36.
27 Christie's London, *Magnificent Jewellery*, 20 June 1990, catalogue no. 205.
28 Ballard, *op. cit.*, p. 61.
29 Kennett, *op. cit.*, p. 100.
30 C. Dior, *Talking About Fashion to Elie Rabourdin and Alice Chavane*, Hutchinson, 1954, p. 21.
31 Charles-Roux, *Chanel, op. cit.*, p. 288.
32 M. Garland, *The Indecisive Decade. The World of Fashion and Entertainment in the Thirties*, Macdonald, 1968, p. 86.
33 Kennett, *op. cit.*, p. 102.
34 Leymarie, *op. cit.*, p. 159.
35 Christie's New York, *Important Jewels*, 25 April 1990, catalogue no. 229; N. Letson, 'The Peerless Verdura', *Connoisseur*, March 1983, p. 54.
36 A. Gold and R. Fizdale, *Misia, The Life of Misia Sert*, Macmillan, 1980, pp. 200–2.
37 Latour, *op. cit.*, p. 191.
38 Garland, *op. cit.*, p. 82; Howell, *op. cit.*, p. 132; F. Kennett, *The Collector's Book of Twentieth-Century Fashion*, Granada, 1983, pp. 31, 38.

Chapter 2

1 Beaton, *op. cit.*, p. 164.
2 S. Menkes, 'Erté: Impossibly Elegant', *International Herald Tribune*, 24 April 1990, p. 8.
3 Sotheby's London, *Chanel at Sotheby's*, 1987, unpaginated.
4 British *Vogue*, Early July 1920, p. 30.
5 Howell, *op. cit.*, p. 26.
6 *Ibid.*, p. 106.
7 Marie, Grand Duchess of Russia, *op. cit.*, pp. 160–1.
8 *Ibid.*, pp. 163, 165–7.
9 N. Adaskina, 'Constructivist Fabrics and Dress Design', *The Journal of Decorative and Propaganda Arts*, No. 5, Summer 1987, pp. 144–59.
10 Marie, Grand Duchess of Russia, *op. cit.*, p. 192.
11 *Ibid.*, pp. 177, 184, 193–5.
12 Charles-Roux, *Chanel and Her World, op. cit.*, p. 197.
13 C. Dior, *Christian Dior's Little Dictionary of Fashion*, Cassell, 1954, p. 15.
14 Howell, *op. cit.*, p. 104.
15 Marie, Grand Duchess of Russia, *op. cit.*, p. 171.
16 M. Battersby, *The Decorative Twenties*, rev. ed., Studio Vista, 1988, p. 146.
17 Howell, *op. cit.*, p. 128.
18 Leymarie, *op. cit.*, p. 126.
19 J. Tregidden, Book Review of *Fashion and Surrealism*, by R. Martin, *Costume*, No. 23, 1989, p. 145.
20 P. White, *Elsa Schiaparelli*, Aurum Books, 1986, p. 92.
21 Garland, *op. cit.*, p. 103; White, *op. cit.*, p. 210; respectively.
22 American *Vogue*, 15 March 1938, p. 83.
23 For a discussion of the Watteau suit see A. Mackrell, *Dress in le style troubadour, 1774–1814*, unpublished Ph.D. thesis, Courtauld Institute of Art, London, 1987, pp. 157–8.
24 S. Menkes, 'Chanel: Lagerfeld's New Look', *International Herald Tribune*, 26 July 1989, p. 9.

Chapter 3

1 Gold and Fizdale, *op. cit.*, p. 197.
2 Charles-Roux, *Chanel, op. cit.*, p. 187.
3 Gold and Fizdale, *op. cit.*, p. 199.
4 B. Kochno, *Diaghilev and the Ballets Russes*, trs. A. Foulke, Allen Lane The Penguin Press, 1971, p. 89.
5 Charles-Roux, *Chanel, op. cit.*, p. 226.
6 A. Mackrell, *The Dress of the Parisian Élégantes, op. cit.*, p. 34.
7 Baillén, *op. cit.*, p. 64.
8 N. de Valois, *Invitation to the Ballet*, John Lane The Bodley Head, 1947, pp. 49–50.
9 L. Sokolova, *Dancing for Diaghilev*, John Murray, 1960, p. 222.
10 *Ibid.*, pp. 222–3.
11 Charles-Roux, *Chanel, op. cit.*, p. 232.
12 *Ibid.*, pp. 229–30.
13 *Ibid*, p. 232.
14 Carter, *op. cit.*, p. 60.
15 F. Steegmuller, *Cocteau: A Biography*, Macmillan, 1970, p. 371.
16 Steegmuller, *op. cit.*, p. 338.
17 Steegmuller, *op. cit.*, p. 389; Leymarie, *op. cit.*, pp. 137–9.
18 Charles-Roux, *Chanel, op. cit.*, p. 268.

19 G. Swanson, *Swanson on Swanson*, Michael Joseph, 1981, pp. 414–15.
20 Marie, Grand Duchess of Russia, *op. cit.*, pp. 172–3.
21 Baillén, *op. cit.*, p. 64.
22 S. Dali, *The Secret Life of Salvador Dali*, Vision, 1973, p. 371.
23 *Ibid.*, pp. 382–3.
24 Evans and Thornton, *op. cit.*, p. 126.
25 Leymarie, *op. cit.*, p. 131.
26 *Ibid.*, p. 199.
27 Gold and Fizdale, *op. cit.*, p. 215.

Chapter 4

1 Ballard, *op. cit.*, p. 64.
2 I. Ashley, 'Coco', in *Paris Fashion. The Great Designers and Their Collections*, ed. R. Lynam, Michael Joseph, 1972, p. 127.
3 *Ibid.*, pp. 127–8.
4 *Ibid.*, pp. 129–30.
5 R. Tredre, 'Discrimination and the elusive taste of Coco', *The Independent*, 9 October 1990, p. 19.
6 Ballard, *op. cit.*, p. 65.
7 *Ibid.*, p. 65.
8 *Ibid.*, p. 65; Kennett, *Coco, op. cit.*, p. 136.
9 Leymarie, *op. cit.*, p. 197.
10 Christie's, London, *The Chanel Wardrobe and Casket of Costume Jewellery, op. cit.*, catalogue no. 63.
11 *Ibid.*, p. 11.
12 Beaton, *op. cit.*, p. 166.

Conclusion

1 Carter, *op. cit.*, p. 66.
2 Ballard, *op. cit.*, p. 65.
3 Kennett, *Coco, op. cit.*, p. 151.
4 S. Menkes, 'A French Model for the 1990s', *International Herald Tribune*, 26 June 1989, p. 20.
5 N. Coleridge, *The Fashion Conspiracy*, Heinemann–Mandarin, 1989, p. 170.
6 S. Menkes, 'Hourglass Chanel Wins for Lagerfeld', *International Herald Tribune*, 24 January 1990, p. 5.
7 *Ibid.*

GLOSSARY

Bouclé French for buckled or curled. Used to describe a woven or knitted surface that has curls and knots.

Ciré French for waxed. Process that involved treating a fabric such as satin with wax, heat and pressure to produce a lustrous, smooth, shiny surface. The material is seen only in black.

Cloqué French for blistered. A fabric with an irregularly raised, embossed surface.

Crêpe a semi-transparent material with a crinkled surface.

Crêpe de Chine a very soft China silk crêpe, plain or figured, woven from a silk warp and worsted thread.

Gore a triangular-shaped panel in a skirt, adding width at the hem without increasing fullness at the waist.

Grosgrain a firm, ribbed fabric, usually made of silk, of warp-faced plain weave with either a matt or slightly shiny surface. The ribs originate from a fine warp coupled with a heavier weft.

Lamé a material interwoven with gold or silver threads.

Ombré a colour which shades in tone.

Organza a sheer, plain-weave fabric with a stiff finish.

Piqué a firm fabric, usually made of cotton, with a raised rib.

Selvedge the edge of the material so woven as to prevent unravelling.

Shirring gathering fabric into rows to decorate part of a garment, notably the bodice, sleeves or yoke.

Taffeta a smooth, lustrous plain or patterned stiff silk fabric.

Tricot French for knitted fabric – a soft flexible material. In the early 1900s, it was in the class of humble materials distinctively associated with Normandy fishermen.

Tulle a gossamer silk net. Named after the French city of Tulle where the material was first made.

BIBLIOGRAPHY

BIOGRAPHIES/FASHION MONOGRAPHS ON
CHANEL

BAILLÉN, C., *Chanel Solitaire*, trs. B. Bray, Collins, 1973.

CHARLES-ROUX, E., *Chanel*, trs. N. Amphoux, Collins
Harvill, 1989.
Chanel and Her World, Weidenfeld & Nicolson,
1982.

HAEDRICH, M., *Coco Chanel – Her Life, Her Secrets*, trs.
C.L. Markmann, Robert Hale & Co., 1972.

KENNETT, F., *Coco. The Life and Loves of Gabrielle Chanel*,
Victor Gollancz, 1989.

LEYMARIE, J., *Chanel*, Skira, 1987.

MADSEN, A., *Coco Chanel: A Biography*, Bloomsbury,
1990.

MORAND, P., *L'Allure de Chanel*, Hermann, 1976.

MEMOIRS, DIARIES, STUDIES WITH
REFERENCES TO CHANEL

BUCKLE, R., *Diaghilev*, Weidenfeld & Nicolson, 1979.

COLETTE, S.D., *Prisons et paradis*, Hachette, 1935.

DALI, S., *The Secret Life of Salvador Dali*, 4th ed., Vision,
1973.

DIOR, C., *Dior by Dior. The Autobiography of Christian
Dior*, trs. A. Fraser, Weidenfeld & Nicolson, 1957.

GOLD, A. & FIZDALE, R., *Misia. The Life of Misia Sert*,
Macmillan, 1980.

KOCHNO, B., *Diaghilev and the Ballets Russes*, trs. A.
Foulke, Allen Lane The Penguin Press, 1971.

SOKOLOVA, L., *Dancing for Diaghilev*, John Murray,
1960.

STEEGMULLER, F., *Cocteau: A Biography*, Macmillan,
1970.

FASHION MONOGRAPHS AND ARTICLES
WITH REFERENCES TO CHANEL

BALLARD, B., *In My Fashion*, Secker & Warburg, 1960.

BATTERSBY, M., *The Decorative Twenties*, rev. ed., Studio
Vista, 1988.

BEATON, C., *The Glass of Fashion*, facsimile ed., Cassell,
1989.

BOUCHER, F., *A History of Costume in the West*, new
enlarged ed., Thames & Hudson, 1987.

BYRDE, P., *A Visual History of Costume: The Twentieth
Century*, B.T. Batsford, 1986.

CARTER, E., *Magic Names of Fashion*, Weidenfeld &
Nicolson, 1980.

COLERIDGE, N., *The Fashion Conspiracy*, Heinemann-
Mandarin, 1989.

DIOR, C., *Talking About Fashion*, Hutchinson, 1954.

EVANS, C. & THORNTON, M., *Women and Fashion. A New
Look*, Quartet Books, 1989.

EWING, E., *History of Twentieth-Century Fashion*, 3rd ed.,
Batsford, 1986.

GARLAND, M., *The Indecisive Decade. The World of
Fashion and Entertainment in the Thirties*,
Macdonald, 1968.

GINSBERG, M., *Paris Fashions. The Art Deco Style of the
1920s*, Bracken Books, 1989.

GLYNN, P., *In Fashion. Dress in the Twentieth Century*,
George Allen & Unwin, 1978.

HOLLANDER, A., 'The Great Emancipator Chanel',
Connoisseur, February 1983.

HOWELL, G., *In Vogue. Sixty Years of Celebrities and
Fashion from British Vogue*, Penguin Books, 1978.

KENNETT, F., *The Collector's Book of Twentieth-Century
Fashion*, Granada, 1983.
Secrets of the Couturiers, Exeter Books, 1984.

LEE-POTTER, C., *Sportswear in Vogue since 1910*, Thames
& Hudson, 1984.

LYNAM, R., ed., *Paris Fashion. The Great Designers and
Their Creations: 'Coco' by I. Ashley*, Michael Joseph,
1972.

MARTIN, R., *Fashion and Surrealism*, Thames & Hudson,
1988.

MARTIN, R. & KODA, H., *The Historical Mode. Fashion and
Art in the 1980s*, Rizzoli, 1989.

MCDOWELL, C., *McDowell's Directory of Twentieth-Century
Fashion*, 2nd rev. ed., Frederick Muller, 1987.

MULVAGH, J., *Costume Jewelry in Vogue*, Thames &
Hudson, 1988.

O'HARA, G., *The Encyclopedia of Fashion*, Thames &
Hudson, 1989.

PERSCHETZ, L., ed., *W, the Designing Life*, Clarkson N.
Potter, 1987.

VREELAND, D., *Inventive Paris Clothes 1900–1939*,
Thames & Hudson, 1977.

WHITE, P., *Elsa Schiaparelli: Empress of Paris Fashion*,
Aurum Books, 1986.

WILSON, E. & TAYLOR, L., *Through the Looking Glass: A
History of Fashion from 1860 to the Present Day*,
BBC Books, 1989.

MUSEUMS WITH CHANEL COLLECTIONS

UNITED KINGDOM

Bath

Museum of Costume

Evening coat of yellow silk damask, 1930s.
Mlle Chanel's working overall of white raised piqué, 1960s.

Castle Howard, York

Costume Galleries

Mlle Chanel's working overall of white piqué, 1960s, (similar to the example in Bath but of flatter piqué).
Suit of brown printed velvet with gilt buttons in the form of a coiled chain, belt applied with filigree crosses and buckle with matching hat and beige silk blouse with side buttoning, c.1961.
Navy blue wool suit with blue and gold buttons, with white cotton blouse, cuff links and petersham bow, c.1960.
Burgundy silk chiffon scarf, 1960s.

London
Theatre Museum
Bathing costumes for *Le Train bleu*, 1924.

Victoria and Albert Museum
Black beaded evening dress, 1919. Straight sleeveless tunic with embroidered bands in a grape design.
Black beaded evening dress, c.1922. Sleeveless dress of georgette, the low-waisted bodice embroidered with curved bead motifs and the slightly flaring skirt with embroidered bands. Black silk drapes trim the sides of the skirt.
Black sequin evening ensemble. Dress and cape, 1936–7. With scarlet satin drapes knotted across the bodice and down the flaring skirt. The short matching semi-circular cape is lined with scarlet satin.
Cream lace evening gown, c.1937.
Black sequin evening suit. Bolero jacket and straight trousers, 1937–8. *En suite* with a blouse of cream chiffon with soft turned-down collar and jabot trimmed with lace.
Scarlet evening gown, c.1939. With grosgrain bodice and peplum, silk chiffon skirt.
Tweed suit, 1960s.
The following collection belonged to Anne Gunning and was given to the V&A in her memory by Sir Anthony Nutting.
Woollen bouclé and woollen jersey suit, 1960s.
Knitted black wool jacket, 1960s.
Beige wool and mohair cardigan, 1960s.
Black wool coat, 1960s.
Black and white woollen tweed bouclé coat, 1960s.
Two cream silk blouses, 1960s.
Black lace, strapless evening gown, 1960s.
Five printed silk scarves, 1960s.
Cream felt beret, 1960s.
Scarlet wool suit, 1960. The semi-fitted jacket has a tailored collar and button trimmed pockets at bust and hips.
Lilac wool suit, 1964. The semi-fitted jacket is lined with lilac floral printed organza which faces the small step lapels, the breast and hip pockets and is used for the bodice attached to the suit skirt.
Black worsted crêpe suit, mid-1960s. Jacket, belted dress and hat.
Day Ensemble, 1987. Dress and jacket of wool bouclé and wool jersey. Karl Lagerfeld for Chanel.
Evening ensemble. Long *robe* of satin and beaded embroidery with a matching satin mini-skirt. Winter 1990. Karl Lagerfeld for Chanel.

FRANCE

Paris

Bibliothèque et Musée de l'Opéra

Costumes for *Le Train bleu*, 1924.

Musée de la Mode et du Costume – Palais Galliera

Ivory muslin Summer gown, c.1922, the corsage applied with vertical bands of Valenciennes lace above horizontal lace edged tiers.

Afternoon dress of black woollen lace with silver decoration, c.1924.

Beige jersey jacket, c.1926, with woven brown and black beige striped collar, cuffs and edging.

Afternoon ensemble. Dress and coat. The dress in *mousseline de soie* printed with a design of Autumn leaves; the coat in green wool with a vandyke collar appliquéd with Autumn leaves.

Printed muslin Summer outfit, c.1929–30. Sleeveless dress and jacket, with a design of Wedgwood blue polka dots on a white ground.

White organza day dress, c.1955–6, embroidered with scarlet and white fishes, scarlet satin trim.

Anthracite black plastic plush suit, late 1960s, with ivory satin lapels and sleeveless blouse.

Vibrantly coloured tweed suit, c.1965, woven overall in predominantly lilac and pink, with repeat chevron designs; complete with hat.

Musée des Arts de la Mode – Union Française des Arts du Costume

Gold and silver lamé bandeau, early twentieth century.

Black lace gown, c.1925, falling in three tiers.

Scarlet velvet evening mantle, c.1925, with deep collar, cut to rest on hips, sunburst seam arrangement to the front.

Jewelled chiffon evening dress, c.1925, emblazoned overall with emerald, ruby and gold pastes and beads.

Black silk crêpe coat, c.1928. Bias cut with interlocking horizontal bands, zig-zag edging, lined in beige silk with similar designs to the inside.

Black satin evening coat, c.1930, with a deep triple collar.

Black lace evening gown, c.1930, falling in tiers, simple tie to the corsage.

Black satin evening gown, c.1938, the black net ground applied overall with tongues of satin ribbon.

Black sequinned sheath, c.1930–5, the corsage ruched and delicately overlaid with black muslin.

Plaid jersey ensemble, c.1930–5.

Loose jacket, waistcoat and calf-length skirt.

Burgundy–coloured lace evening gown, c. 1930, falling in three tiers.

Black tulle evening gown, c.1935–8, with balloon-sleeves emphasized by shoulder flounces, diamanté buttons to corsage, full skirt.

Sapphire blue 'firework' gown, c.1938, full-length, the tulle ground applied overall with petrol blue sequins in cascading firework designs.

Crêpe georgette evening gown, c.1938–9, printed overall with white spots, separately appliquéd polka-dot trim.

Red georgette dinner gown, c.1956, with cross-over bodice above horizontal banding, floating panels to the arms.

White and gold organza dinner gown, c.1958, with fitted corsage, overall design of gold spots, puffball skirt.

White organza gown, c.1958, with blue and white silk boned corsage adorned with large striped bow, striped band to hem over stiffened petticoats.

Pink lace gown, c.1958, the boned corsage adorned with a navy blue bow.

Blue and white tweed suit, c.1959, of Prince of Wales tweed with gingham blouse and trim.

Black and gold flecked evening gown, c.1959, shirred overall and embellished with bold black and gold bows and ribbons.

Ivory georgette evening gown, c.1957, with round neckline, short cape attached to shoulders, the skirt falling in three tiered drape flounces.

Ivory lace gown, c.1958, with boned strapless bodice, full skirt over stiffened petticoats.

Cream and wool bouclé wool suit, c.1960, with fuchsia silk blouse.

Rose tweed suit, c.1960, with gold lamé sleeveless blouse.

White tweed coat, c.1960, lined with Mongolian lamb.

Pink tweed hat, c.1960.

Navy blue dinner dress, c.1960, of tiered pleated chiffon, with large taffeta bow to the rear.

Textured ivory wool suit with fringed trim, c.1960.

Bouclé tweed suit, c.1965, of flecked grey and rust tweed with dark brown borders.

Plum chenille and gold lurex suit, 1965, comprising sleeveless dress with peach bodice, plum jacket.

Pink and silver brocaded dress and velvet coat, c.1967. The dress brocaded overall with Chanel logo repeats under a black velvet coat.

Black organza evening gown, 1967, with flounced fichu neckline, the skirt falling in four tiers.

White silk and silver lurex trouser suit, 1967, with overall textured trellis design, fastened by three buttons and loops.

Sequinned outfit, 1968, comprising a bodice over full

short skirt, and pantaloons of brocaded lurex in pink, green and lilac, bordered by opalescent sequins and bronze fringes.

Pink sequinned velvet trouser suit, *c.*1968, the pink sequinned top with deep collar, black bow, black bouclé wool trousers.

Black and pink evening ensemble, *c.*1968. Sleeveless dress and jacket with an overall harlequin design of black sequins on a pink ground.

Grey and pink jersey suit, 1968, with rose-pink blouse and contrasting piping and buttons.

Gold and black velour trouser suit, 1970. Tunic top woven with black and gold flowerheads, black velvet trousers and cravat.

UNITED STATES OF AMERICA

Los Angeles

Los Angeles County Museum of Art

Black crêpe dress with multi-coloured embroidery, *c.*1922.

Beaded evening dress, 1925.

Pink georgette evening dress, 1925.

Burgundy velveteen coat, 1925.

Black silk dress, 1925.

Ecru lace dinner dress, 1925.

White chiffon, beaded evening dress, 1920s.

Cream silk jacket with fur collar and cuffs, early 1930s.

Navy blue lace evening dress, *c.*1932.

Black and white polka dot crêpe afternoon dress, 1933.

Brown wool, Persian lamb coat, *c.*1933.

Black and white cotton lace evening dress, 1936.

Navy blue wool jersey dress, *c.*1938.

Navy blue wool tweed suit, 1954.

Pink, blue and white tweed suit, 1958.

Gold embroidered lace evening dress, *c.*1959.

Navy and white wool tweed suit, 1959–60

Pale blue wool cocktail ensemble, embellished with sequins, early 1960s.

White wool suit, early 1960s.

Gold silk/black moiré suit, early 1960s. With shoes.

Navy blue shantung suit, 1962.

Coral and black wool tweed dress, *c.*1962.

Black and white wool tweed suit, *c.*1962.

Yellow wool suit, 1964.

Black and white plaid wool suit, 1964.

Black and white mohair suit, 1964. With shoes and handbag.

Pink and white mohair coat and dress, 1965.

Coffee, taupe and white tweed suit, 1965.

Green silk and gold lamé cocktail dress and jacket, mid-1960s.

Raspberry silk chiffon afternoon dress, 1966.

Orange and black wool tweed suit, 1966.

Black and white wool tweed suit, 1966.

Pink silk organza cocktail dress, 1967.

Silk suit, with a print in earth colours, *c.*1971.

New York

Metropolitan Museum of Art – Costume Institute

Black dancing dress, 1926–7, with gold metallic lace arranged in geometrically patterned stripes and trimmed with gold and black sequins. It is short and cut straight, with a flared flounce at the hemline.

Black and ivory silk charmeuse suit, *c.*1927.

Black wool jersey and black satin day ensemble, *c.*1927.

Theatre coat in white and black *ombré* silk, *c.*1927.

Day ensemble, *c.*1927. Dress and coat. Dress of silk chiffon printed in cerise, orange and black; coat of yellow and grey wool tweed lined in the dress fabric.

Blue linen suit, 1937.

Gypsy dress, *c.*1939. Full skirt, long-sleeved lace blouse, with a wide Roman-striped taffeta ribbon sash.

Black, blue and azure tweed suit, *c.*1955.

Philadelphia

Museum of Art

Navy blue wool jersey coat, *c.*1930. Fitted princess line; inverted pleat at back hem. Matching silk crêpe lining in upper half of garment.

Dress and jacket, *c.*1960. Blue-grey, grey, brown, blue, lavender tweed novelty weave wool, and navy and shaded grey silk. The jacket has a mandarin collar and is box cut. The sleeveless dress has a jewel neckline and a dropped waist with a sash.

Yellow and grey wool suit, trimmed with braided self-material, 1963–5; with a blouse of yellow silk.

Dress and jacket, 1964. Blue, green, pink and tan checked wool, with metallic bodice and lining.

Black and white plaid wool suit, trimmed with black

and white wool bands, 1964–6.

Wool suit, 1965.

Dress and jacket, c.1965. Pink, mustard and gold brocade; jacket lined in variegated pink and metallic knit.

Cream on cream wool tweed suit, in a checked pattern top-stitched in bars. With a blouse of matching silk with decorative top-stitched bias at the front and a jewel neckline; and a scarf in matching silk with pointed ends.

Wheat-coloured wool suit, with bands of braided gold tape, c.1968.

Beige silk dress with a matching sash, c.1968.

Blue-grey, white and tan basketweave wool coat, lined in beige silk, c.1968.

Trouser suit, c.1970. Green and red printed gauze brocaded in gold.

Jumpsuit and jacket, c.1970. Light beige and gold silk brocade. The jumpsuit has a sleeveless, fitted bodice, full straight trousers attached to the bodice at the waist with narrow gold braid.

Burgundy silk velvet suit, c.1975. Jacket and two skirts. With two blouses of sheer pink silk gauze.

San Francisco

Fine Arts Museums

Evening dress, c.1935. Full-length, sleeveless dress with fitted bodice and gored skirt of royal blue silk tulle machine embroidered with white stars, worn over underdress of blue silk crêpe with inset bands of white and blue tulle at hem. Matching embroidered tulle capelet and sash.

Short evening dress, attributed to Chanel, c.1956. Slim, strapless dress of black silk crêpe chiffon over black silk; self-cord belt and attached flowing shoulder scarf/stole.

Pink angora wool twill suit, c.1960. With polychrome chiné-printed silk taffeta blouse with self-tie at neck.

Red-ribbed wool knit cardigan suit, 1960s. With long-sleeved blouse of ivory silk crêpe with detachable self-tie at neck.

Blue, white and fuchsia striped wool suit, c.1964. With orange and fuchsia sleeveless blouse.

Brown, white and beige striped wool suit, c.1964. With sleeveless blouse of tan silk crêpe.

CHRONOLOGY

1883	Born 19 August Gabrielle Bonheur Chanel in Saumur, Auvergne.	1905–8	Café-concert singer, nicknamed 'Coco', in Moulins and in Vichy.
1895–1900	Educated at convent orphanage run by the Sisters of the Congregation of the Sacred Heart of Mary at Aubazine.	1908–9	Lived with Etienne Balsan at his Château de Royallieu and in Paris.
1900–2	Educated at convent school in Moulins.	1909–10	Established millinery shop in the boulevard Malesherbes, Paris.
1900–4	Worked as an assistant in a small shop specializing in trousseaux and layettes and also in a tailor shop in Moulins.	1910	With the sponsorship of Arthur ('Boy') Capel (died 1919) established millinery salon at 21 rue Cambon, Paris. Licensed

1912   as a *modiste*.

1912   Designed hats for the actress, Gabrielle Dorizat, to wear in F. Nozière's play *Bel Ami*, Théâtre de Vaudeville, Paris. Hats illustrated in *Les Modes*.

1913–15   Established fashion shop in Deauville selling clothes as well as millinery.

1915–20   Established Chanel-Biarritz, a *maison de couture*, in Biarritz.

1916   Returned to 21 rue Cambon, Paris.

1919   Officially registered as a *couturière* and established *maison de couture* at 31 rue Cambon, Paris, where the House of Chanel is located today.

1920   Met Grand Duke Dmitri of Russia. Has brief liaison.

1921   Launched Chanel No. 5.

1922   Designed costumes for Jean Cocteau's play *Antigone*, Théâtre de l'Atelier, Paris.

1924   Parfums Chanel established. Opens jewellery workshop.

1924   Designed costumes for Serge Diaghilev's and Jean Cocteau's *opérette-dansée Le Train bleu*, Théâtre des Champs-Elysées, Paris. Associated with the 2nd Duke of Westminster (to 1931).

1926   Designed costumes for Jean Cocteau's play *Orphée*.

1928   Founded Tricots Chanel, re-named Tissus Chanel, at Asnières.

1929   Designed costumes for Igor Stravinsky's ballet *Apollo Musagètes*, Théâtre Sarah Bernhardt, Paris.

1931   Designed costumes for Gloria Swanson to wear in the film *Tonight or Never*.

1932   Exhibition of Chanel authentic diamond jewellery designs, at her private salons, rue du Faubourg Saint-Honoré, Paris. Benefit show of one hundred and thirty Chanel costume designs, at the apartments of the Duke of Westminster, Grosvenor Square, London.

1932–6   Lived with Paul Iribe.

1934   'Marianne', the symbol of the French Republic, in the likeness of Coco Chanel, cover design by Iribe for *Le Témoin*, 14 October.

1936   Wrote 'When Fashion Illustrates History', article in the *Revue des sports et du monde*, June–July.

1937   Designed costumes for Jean Cocteau's play *Oedipe roi*, Théâtre Antoine, Paris. Designed costumes for Jean Cocteau's play *Les Chevaliers du table ronde*, Théâtre de l'Oeuvre, Paris.

1938   Designed costumes for Jean Renoir's film *La Marseillaise*.

1939   Designed costumes for Salvador Dali's ballet *Bacchanale*, Ballets Russes de Monte Carlo
Closed *maison de couture*, 31 rue Cambon, Paris, on the declaration of World War II on 3 September, leaving open only her boutique of accessories and perfumes.

1941–4   Lived with German officer, Hans Gunther von Dincklage ('Spatz').

1945–53   Moved to Switzerland, living alternately in Lausanne and Paris.

1954   5 February. Comeback.

1957   Received Neiman Marcus Award, Dallas, Texas.

1961   Designed the costumes for Alain Resnais's film *Last Year at Marienbad*.

1963   Received *The Sunday Times* International Fashion Award, London.

1969   *Coco*, a Broadway musical based on her life with the costumes designed by Cecil Beaton.

1971   10 January, died in Paris.
Gaston Berthelot appointed designer at the House of Chanel.

1977   Decision to make ready-to-wear at the House of Chanel. Philippe Guibourgé appointed to design the ready-to-wear collections.

1978   2 December. The Chanel Wardrobe and Casket of Costume Jewellery, sale of the personal collection of Chanel, at Christie's London.

1983   Karl Lagerfeld appointed design director for both the ready-to-wear and the couture lines at the House of Chanel.

1987   5–13 September. Exhibition: Chanel at Sotheby's London.

INDEX